TIM WATERMAN

THE FUNDAMENTALS OF LANDSCAPE ARCHITECTURE

ava | Academia
the environment of learning

An AVA Book
Published by AVA Publishing SA
Rue des Fontenailles 16
Case Postale
1000 Lausanne 6
Switzerland
Tel: +41 786 005 109
Email: enquiries@avabooks.ch

Distributed by Thames & Hudson
(ex-North America)
181a High Holborn
London WC1V 7QX
Tel: +44 20 7845 5000
Fax: +44 20 7845 5055
Email: sales@thameshudson.co.uk
www.thamesandhudson.com

Distributed in the USA & Canada by:
Ingram Publisher Services Inc
1 Ingram Blvd
La Vergne, TN 37086
USA
Tel: +1 866 400 5351
Fax: +1 800 838 1149
Email: customer.service@
ingrampublisherservices.com

English Language Support Office
AVA Publishing (UK) Ltd
Tel: +44 1903 204 455
Email: enquiries@avabooks.co.uk

Design by Anne Odling-Smee, O-SB Design

Cover image by Latz + Partner

Production by
AVA Book Production Pte. Ltd
Singapore
Tel: +65 6334 8173
Fax: +65 6259 9830
Email: production@avabooks.com.sg

All reasonable attempts have been made
to trace, clear and credit the copyright
holders of the images reproduced in this
book. However, if any credits have been
inadvertently omitted, the publisher will
endeavour to incorporate amendments in
future editions.

ISBN 978-2-940373-91-8
10 9 8 7 6 5 4 3 2 1

THE FUNDAMENTALS OF LANDSCAPE ARCHITECTURE

TIM WATERMAN

CONTENTS

HOW TO GET THE MOST OUT OF THIS BOOK

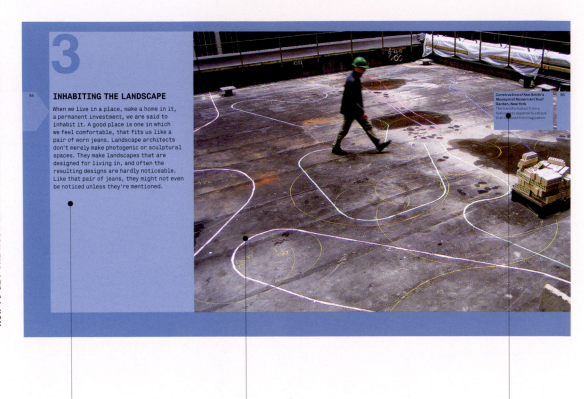

3

64

INHABITING THE LANDSCAPE

When we live in a place, make a home in it,
a permanent investment, we are said to
inhabit it. A good place is one in which
we feel comfortable, that fits us like a
pair of worn jeans. Landscape architects
don't merely make photogenic or sculptural
spaces. They make landscapes that are
designed for living in, and often the
resulting designs are hardly noticeable.
Like that pair of jeans, they might not even
be noticed unless they're mentioned.

Construction of Ken Smith's
Museum of Modern Art Roof
Garden, New York
The transformation from a
feature is expanse to a place
that captures the imagination.

65

Images
Photographs, diagrams and
illustrations from an array of
professional practices bring the text
to life.

Chapter introductions
Provide a brief outline of the key
concepts and ideas that the chapter
will explore.

Captions
Supply contextual information
about the images and help connect
the visuals with those key concepts
discussed in the body copy.

ORTHOGRAPHIC PROJECTION

Orthographic projection is measured drawing producing a 'true' representation of a site or object that is to scale. It is also called technical drawing. Orthographic projection generally means creating a two-dimensional representation of a three-dimensional site or object. Builders, following instructions from a designer, will consult these accurate drawings so that they know exactly where and how to build each element of a project. The man in the hard hat with the plans in his hands? He's holding an orthographic projection.

A plan is a two-dimensional measured horizontal drawing. It places the viewer in an imaginary position above the site or object looking straight down at it without any distortion. A section is a vertical slice through the site or object, just like a slice of bread. It shows the exact height and width of every object it encounters. It appears on the plan as a simple line where the two planes intersect. Plans and sections are the two primary types of orthographic projections.

SCALE

Scale is the medium through which it is possible to create orthographic projections. It is generally expressed as a fraction or a ratio. It is used to produce a drawing at a specific fraction of the full-size dimensions of an object. A scale drawing at life size would be at a scale of 1:1 or 1/1, whereas a drawing at half life size would be at a ratio of 1:2 or 1/2.

SCALE

The following scales are merely indicative, and are intended only to give a feeling for the range of scales and the size of site to which they would be applied. These scales would produce drawings of presentation or map size.

1:1	Actual size
1:10	Bus shelter
1:100	Garden
1:500	City park
1:1,000	Neighbourhood
1:20,000	City
1:200,000	County
1:1,000,000	Country
1:5,000,000	Europe
1:50,000,000	World

In order to fit a large site on to a standard-sized piece of paper, landscape architects often use much more 'zoomed-out' scales such as 1:200 or 1:1,000. A site at the scale of 1:1,000 would be 1,000 times smaller than life size, and this scale might be used for a project covering a significant area, such as a large housing development. Maps zoom out even further. The city of Florence can be well covered at the scale of 1:12,500, but all of Italy might need a scale of 1:1,000,000.

PLANS

A plan represents the site as it is measured on the surface of the ground, registering the horizontal distances between objects. It is a two-dimensional measured technical drawing. Plans are excellent tools for communicating a design, but are usually very poor tools for the work of design itself. Because they place the viewer in

Section drawings
These simple sections show terraces being built. The dump truck in the image helps establish scale.

an unnatural position, looking straight down on the site from an imaginary height, they lead to a tendency to simply make patterns on the ground, rather than creating three-dimensional spaces for people. Because of this top-down view, they create an illusion of power that reduces the humans in a design scheme to mere pawns in a board game. However, plans are essential to ensure that design proposals explored in other types of drawings are correctly proportioned, fitting on the site in the manner intended.

SECTIONS

A section shows the heights and widths of objects encountered on a vertical slice through the objects appearing on a plan. It is a two-dimensional, measured technical drawing showing the distances between these elements. Beginning with a simple line on the plan, a section is then projected upwards. A section shows only those elements that appear precisely on that line. A section does not show any depth or perspective. Sections are useful to verify that elements shown on a plan are in appropriate human scale, especially when people are included in the drawing. It can be particularly helpful to show a series of sections through a site in parallel, particularly where there is interesting or varied topography. The series builds up a

picture of the site in sequence, which can be very informative. A good landscape architectural section drawing will show elements not merely above ground, but also below.

SECTION ELEVATIONS

Section elevations, often simply called 'elevations', begin with exactly the same principles as a section drawing – with a line on the plan that is projected upwards. A section elevation, however, will show not only those elements that fall directly on the line, but everything appearing behind those elements looking in one direction. The apparent sizes of these objects do not shrink into the distance, as they would in a perspective drawing. They are pictured in exact scale regardless of their distance from the section line. Section elevations can provide a very complete image of a project, and are very useful for testing designs.

Box outs
Contain more detailed and contextual information about those landscape architects or practices that are referred to in the body copy.

Colour coding
Denotes the chapter.

Navigation
Chapter navigation helps you determine which chapter unit you are in and what the preceding and following sections are.

Diagrams
Help to explain landscape architectural theory and concepts in more detail.

INTRODUCTION

'If there's sky, it's mine.'
Kathryn Gustafson,
Landscape architect

WHAT IS LANDSCAPE ARCHITECTURE?

When asked where landscape architects work, many people might point out their back door to the garden. It would be more accurate, however, to look out the front door. The landscape is anywhere and everywhere outdoors, and landscape architects are shaping the face of the Earth across cities, towns and countryside alike. Landscape architecture involves shaping and managing the physical world and the natural systems that we inhabit. Landscape architects do design gardens, but what is critical is that the garden, or any other outdoor space, is seen in context. All living things are interdependent and the landscape is where they all come together. Context is social, cultural, environmental and historical, amongst other considerations. Landscape architects are constantly zooming in and out from the details to the big picture to ensure that balance is maintained.

Landscape architecture combines art and science to make places. The art provides a vision for a landscape, using drawings, models, computer imaging and text. The elements of design, such as line, shape, texture and colour, are used to create these images, and the process allows the designer to both communicate with an audience and to visualise the site in order to act upon it. The science includes an understanding of natural systems, including geology, soils, plants, topography, hydrology, climate and ecology. It also includes a knowledge of structures and how they are built, such as roads and bridges, walls, paving and even the occasional building. Landscape architects are broad thinkers who thrive on the big picture.

Landscape architects are playing an increasingly important role in solving the great issues of our day, such as dealing with climate change and providing sustainable communities. They are working on urban regeneration and master-planning projects, tackling environmental hazards, designing Olympic sites, and creating the public squares, parks and streets we all use.

Landscape architecture is increasingly a field that requires natural leaders who can utilise their wide-ranging knowledge to lead large projects. It still, however, provides plenty of opportunities to make a substantial difference on a smaller scale as well. It is simply not possible to give a satisfactory short definition of landscape architecture, because of the incredible breadth of the field – but far from being a shortcoming, this is landscape architecture's great strength. For those who crave both variety and a challenge, and are curious about everything that makes the world go around, a career in landscape architecture is ideal.

Fresh Kills Lifescape, Staten Island, New York, Field Operations, 2001–2005
Fresh Kills is an artificial topography created by half a century's worth of New York garbage. It shows the great range of landscape architecture in one project, from the need to mitigate pollution, clean groundwater and trap escaping methane while creating a public park for people and wildlife.

WHERE DO LANDSCAPE ARCHITECTS WORK?

Landscape architects work within an incredibly diverse number of places. Anywhere humans have a hand in shaping the landscape, you may find a landscape architect at work. Some may specialise in a specific area, but many will have the opportunity to work with a wide variety of fields over the course of a career.

Everyday places – schoolyards, parks, streets
Monumental places – Olympic campuses, grand public squares, waterfront developments
Play places – resorts, golf courses, playgrounds, theme or amusement parks
Natural places – national parks, wetlands, forests, environmental preserves
Private places – gardens, courtyards, corporate campuses, science or industrial parks

Historic places – historic monuments, heritage landscapes, historic urban areas
Scholarly places – universities, botanic gardens, arboreta
Contemplative places – healing gardens, sensory gardens, cemeteries
Productive places – community gardens, storm water management, agricultural land
Industrial places – factories and industrial development, mining and mine reclamation, reservoirs and hydroelectric installations
Travel places – highways, transportation corridors and structures, bridges
The entire place – new towns, urban regeneration and housing projects

**Courtyard in the LG Chemical
Research Centre, Seoul, Korea**
This courtyard by Mikyoung Kim
derives its contemplative beauty
from the great precision of its design.
A simple, elegant relationship
between bamboo, moss, stone and
water create a highly sculptural
composition.

THE ROLE OF LANDSCAPE ARCHITECTS

As a profession, landscape architecture is relatively new, dating back only about a century and a half. However, the term 'landscape architecture' emerged slightly earlier. It sits within a group of interdependent professions that can be conveniently called 'the architectures', which include: architecture, landscape architecture, interior architecture, urban design and urban planning. There are also significant overlaps with civil engineering, especially in the United States.

Most projects require teams that are composed of representatives from some or all of the architectures. The overlapping nature of the architectures adds to the difficulty in understanding these career paths, as many practitioners are quite comfortable moving across boundaries. Urban design, for example, is not exactly a profession unto itself, but a specialisation of landscape architects, architects and urban planners. It is perhaps simplest to say that landscape architects create places for people to live, work and enjoy, and places for plants and animals to thrive. Landscape architects also speak up for the care and preservation of our landscapes.

Landscape architecture combines social, economic, environmental and cultural perspectives. Landscape architects study, plan, design and manage spaces, which are both sustainable and visually pleasing. They shape the face of the Earth and also help to shape the face of the future.

1

HISTORY AND IDEAS

The history of humankind is written in the landscape. Every civilisation, every empire, has left its mark in some significant way. People have, for millennia, felt the need to build and create, not just to provide for the basic needs of food, shelter and companionship, but to make glorious monuments that symbolise their collective ambitions.

We have, as a species, become disconnected from the landscape that supports us in many ways. For example, we are rarely able to make a link between the food on our plates and the landscape that produced it. This disconnection is also often clear when we look at the great built landscapes of our past. Most people, for instance, see the Pyramids at Giza as merely buildings, but in reality they were parts of a complex functioning landscape. An understanding of the history of landscapes can help us to see the whole picture.

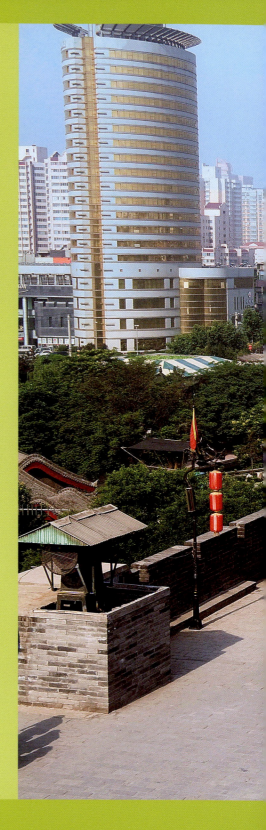

The ancient city wall in Xi'an, China
Contemporary buildings overshadow the ancient city wall, which in turn overshadows a modern streetscape where building façades are a mix of old and new.

YESTERDAY AND TODAY

'What we owe the future is not a new start, for we can only begin with what has happened. We owe the future the past, the long knowledge that is the potency of time to come.'
Wendell Berry

Landscape architecture, as it is practised today, is quite distinct from its historical roots in landscape gardening, and it is on a course that is still evolving. At its most basic level, it is still about building landscapes for inhabitation and sustaining the human species. However, the great advances of knowledge and technology through the last two centuries have completely changed our relationship with the land. One of the greatest paradoxes of our day, perhaps, is that while we have never known more about natural systems, we have never in history done more damage to them. There is now almost no place on Earth that we have not changed or affected in some way. Landscape architecture is increasingly responding to the realisation that we are living in a world that is very much of our own making, and if we are to save it for the future, it will require a great deal more making and less destroying.

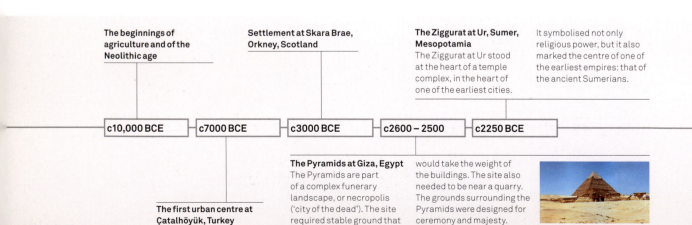

The beginnings of agriculture and of the Neolithic age

Settlement at Skara Brae, Orkney, Scotland

The Ziggurat at Ur, Sumer, Mesopotamia
The Ziggurat at Ur stood at the heart of a temple complex, in the heart of one of the earliest cities.

It symbolised not only religious power, but it also marked the centre of one of the earliest empires: that of the ancient Sumerians.

c10,000 BCE	c7000 BCE	c3000 BCE	c2600 – 2500	c2250 BCE

The first urban centre at Çatalhöyük, Turkey

The Pyramids at Giza, Egypt
The Pyramids are part of a complex funerary landscape, or necropolis ('city of the dead'). The site required stable ground that would take the weight of the buildings. The site also needed to be near a quarry. The grounds surrounding the Pyramids were designed for ceremony and majesty.

People have always left their mark on the landscape, from the earliest cave paintings to great feats of engineering such as Stonehenge. While we shape landscapes, we are at the same time the product of these places. In an urbanised world, we are more and more the product of city landscapes. As with rural landscapes, no two cities are alike. A forest dweller is as different from a desert nomad as a Parisian is from an Athenian.

It is in the landscape that all the interconnected forces of our existence come together. The ability to arrive at an enlightened design and strategy that recognises the uniqueness of individual places while understanding their place in larger systems is thus a crucial skill. Landscape architecture is growing to meet this challenge – it is building upon its past to create a better future for all.

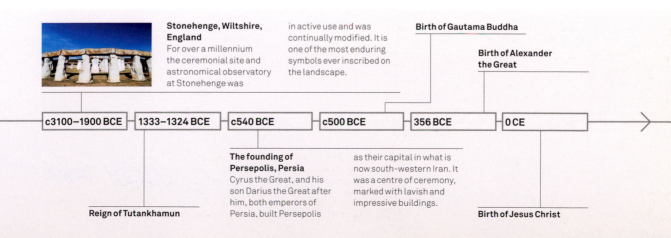

Stonehenge, Wiltshire, England
For over a millennium the ceremonial site and astronomical observatory at Stonehenge was in active use and was continually modified. It is one of the most enduring symbols ever inscribed on the landscape.

Birth of Gautama Buddha

Birth of Alexander the Great

| c3100–1900 BCE | 1333–1324 BCE | c540 BCE | c500 BCE | 356 BCE | 0 CE |

Reign of Tutankhamun

The founding of Persepolis, Persia
Cyrus the Great, and his son Darius the Great after him, both emperors of Persia, built Persepolis as their capital in what is now south-western Iran. It was a centre of ceremony, marked with lavish and impressive buildings.

Birth of Jesus Christ

BEFORE THE ANCIENT WORLD

THE DAWN OF CIVILISATION

The earliest humans would have led exceptionally busy lives. Hunting and gathering would have occupied most of their time and energy – tracking animals and searching for plants bearing edible roots, fruit or leaves. They would have had to wander far and wide for a meagre dinner, with only occasional bounty. The marks they made on the landscape may have been as small as footprints or discarded bones and shells. It is difficult to say just how much sense of belonging the early humans might have felt in the landscape.

As agriculture emerged around 12,000 years ago, fixed settlements of people became more common. It is easier to imagine that people might have given names to the hills and rivers that gave shape to their existence, which provided them with more stable sustenance. Skara Brae on the windswept Orkney Islands to the north of Scotland is the most complete Stone Age settlement in Europe, built roughly 5,000 years ago.

'When we dream alone it is only a dream, but when many dream together it is the beginning of a new reality.'
Friedensreich Hundertwasser

What is startling about Skara Brae is just how recognisable it is that people were making a home, making a place, in more or less the same way we do now.

Stonehenge in Wiltshire, England, and the great field of standing stones at Carnac in Brittany, France, are monumental examples of how Stone Age people left their mark on the land.

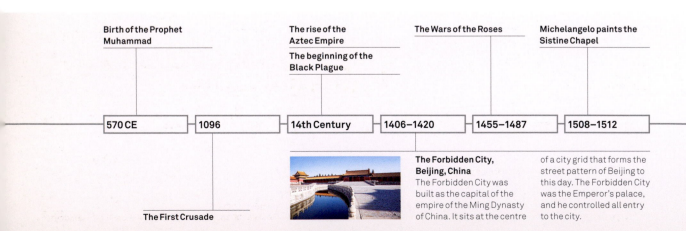

Birth of the Prophet Muhammad		The rise of the Aztec Empire / The beginning of the Black Plague		The Wars of the Roses		Michelangelo paints the Sistine Chapel
570 CE	1096	14th Century	1406–1420	1455–1487	1508–1512	

The First Crusade

The Forbidden City, Beijing, China
The Forbidden City was built as the capital of the empire of the Ming Dynasty of China. It sits at the centre of a city grid that forms the street pattern of Beijing to this day. The Forbidden City was the Emperor's palace, and he controlled all entry to the city.

The neolithic settlement of Skara Brae in the Orkney Islands, Scotland
Skara Brae was continually occupied for approximately 600 years. The buildings were nestled into heaps of old kitchen rubbish called middens, which provided shelter and insulation for the buildings from the harsh North Sea climate.

The gardens at the Villa d'Este, Tivoli, Italy
The Villa d'Este is a masterpiece of Renaissance Italian garden design. It is a highly romanticised image of the natural world, and is notable for its very elaborate gravity-fed fountains.

Vaux-le-Vicomte, near Melun, France
André le Nôtre designed the impeccable landscape at Vaux-le-Vicomte, a masterpiece of baroque design that incited such jealousy in Louis XIV that he hired the same designer to create the ultimate garden for him at Versailles.

| 1550 | 1564 | 1620 | 1633 | 1661 | 1666 |

Shalimar Bagh, Kashmir, India
Elaborate fountains and cascades over three levels were constructed in the beautiful Shalimar Gardens of the Shah Jahan. The gardens were arranged in a grid pattern, much like Shah Jahan's most famous creation, the Taj Mahal.

Birth of William Shakespeare

Inquisition trial of Galileo Galilei

The Great Fire of London

WESTERN CIVILISATIONS

The 'cradle of civilisation' was more central than western. Mesopotamia, the rich but vast and featureless valleys of the Tigris and Euphrates (now present-day Iraq), were farmed by the Sumerians, the culture that preceded the Babylonians. The Sumerians built great brick ziggurats – stepped pyramids rising high out of the level plain. Some archaeologists believe that the terraces of these huge structures were planted with trees and gardens. These massive pyramids would have helped to organise the otherwise bland landscape as landmarks – markers of place and identity.

The floodwaters of the Nile River in Africa nourished the land with silts and sediments in much the same way as the Tigris and Euphrates, and the civilisation of ancient Egypt took root in the fertile plains.

The great ambitions and power of the pharaohs made it possible for the Pyramids at Giza to be built, as well as the remarkable temple at Karnak and the tombs at Luxor.

Mediterranean civilisation was soon to shift north from Egypt to ancient Greece, and then to Rome, where the philosophies underpinning our world views were first articulated.

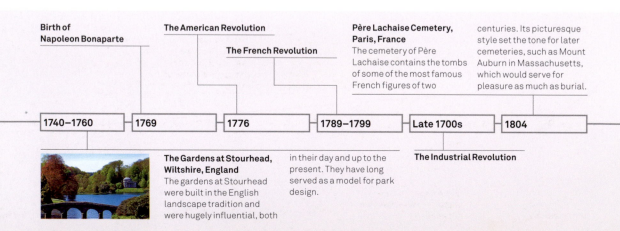

Birth of Napoleon Bonaparte

The American Revolution

The French Revolution

Père Lachaise Cemetery, Paris, France
The cemetery of Père Lachaise contains the tombs of some of the most famous French figures of two

centuries. Its picturesque style set the tone for later cemeteries, such as Mount Auburn in Massachusetts, which would serve for pleasure as much as burial.

1740–1760	1769	1776	1789–1799	Late 1700s	1804

The Gardens at Stourhead, Wiltshire, England
The gardens at Stourhead were built in the English landscape tradition and were hugely influential, both

in their day and up to the present. They have long served as a model for park design.

The Industrial Revolution

The temple complex at Karnak near Luxor, Egypt
A sphinx-lined avenue connects two of the temples at Karnak. The great complexity of the site takes it out of the realm of building architecture into landscape architecture and urbanism. The entire complex is a walled enclosure with interior spaces that include buildings and garden courtyards. The processional routes between the temples foreshadow the great avenues that were to come.

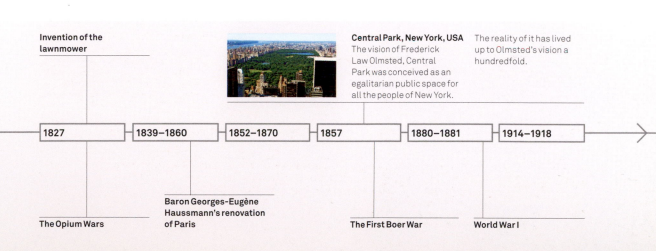

Invention of the lawnmower

Central Park, New York, USA
The vision of Frederick Law Olmsted, Central Park was conceived as an egalitarian public space for all the people of New York.

The reality of it has lived up to Olmsted's vision a hundredfold.

| 1827 | 1839–1860 | 1852–1870 | 1857 | 1880–1881 | 1914–1918 |

Baron Georges-Eugène Haussmann's renovation of Paris

The Opium Wars

The First Boer War

World War I

EASTERN CIVILISATIONS

The evolution of humans in the landscape followed much the same progress in the Far East as it did in the West. The earliest hunter-gatherers improved their circumstances through the domestication of animals and the development of agricultural practice. The links between West and East are perhaps more profound than is commonly imagined. The prehistoric development of Eurasian languages are linked in ways that suggest that nomadic tribes had spheres of influence that overlapped across all of Europe and Asia. These tribes would have travelled with domesticated animals and lived an itinerant existence, following resources seasonally across the landscape.

Almost everywhere in the East, there are remains to be found that are strikingly similar to those found in Europe. These include standing stones, either in circles or alone, and dolmens. For much of the history of humankind, many of the most important marks made upon the landscape were in commemoration of death. There has been much speculation over the years about the uses of these stones, and aside from their use as tomb markers, it seems most likely that the stones either had spiritual significance or they were used as observatories. One thing is certain: they served to fix a place in the landscape that signified a belonging, which marked a physical place on the planet, as well as a location within the cosmos. It is this significance that has resonance and relevance to us today; it situates the work of landscape architects within human needs and aspirations, which stretch back over millennia.

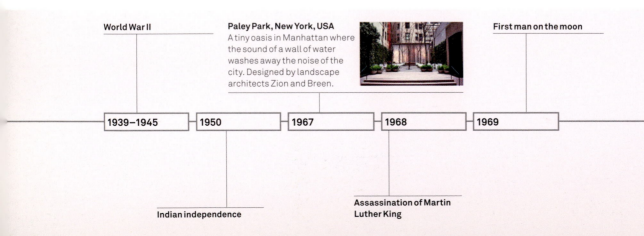

World War II

Paley Park, New York, USA
A tiny oasis in Manhattan where the sound of a wall of water washes away the noise of the city. Designed by landscape architects Zion and Breen.

First man on the moon

| 1939–1945 | 1950 | 1967 | 1968 | 1969 |

Indian independence

Assassination of Martin Luther King

Standing stones in the Altai Mountains, Siberia
The Altai Mountains are in the centre of Asia, at the meeting point of Siberia, Kazakhstan and Mongolia. The stones protrude starkly from the vast, windswept steppe.

End of the Vietnam War   Berlin Wall dismantled   War in Iraq

| 1970 | 1975 | 1989 | 2003 | 2008 |

Copacabana Beach, Rio de Janeiro, Brazil
Bold modernist patterns, including the emblematic wave motif that unifies the waterfront along

Copacabana Beach, are typical of the work of Roberto Burle Marx. His exuberant landscapes captured the optimistic spirit of the age.

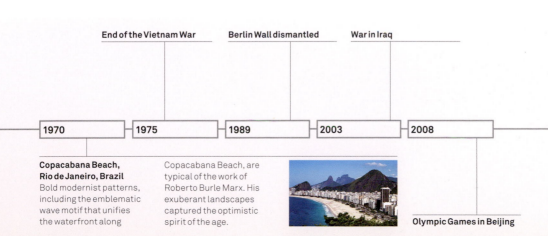

Olympic Games in Beijing

THE ANCIENT WORLD

Gods and monarchs gave shape to the landscapes of the ancient world, which were often built on a scale that is still impressive today. A great flowering of knowledge and culture happened all over the world, more or less simultaneously, over the space of roughly 1,000 years. The society of ancient Greece brought us the science and philosophy that still provide the foundation of western culture, as well as great landscapes such as the Acropolis at Athens. Roman culture spread across Europe and Africa by dint of force and introduced new techniques of building. It also left behind new patterns of city development and impressive infrastructure from roads to aqueducts.

In the East, amazing structures such as the stupas (reliquaries) at Borobudur in Indonesia, and Sanchi in India, mark the emergence of Buddhism. In present-day Iran, the ruined city of Persepolis marks the heart of the mighty Persian Empire.

The cultures in Pre-Columbian America created cities every bit as astounding as those anywhere else in the world, from the Sun Pyramid at Teotihuacan, the palace and temples of the Mayan city of Palenque, to the Incan city of Machu Picchu. Although the Incas were contemporary with the Middle Ages in Europe, they are perhaps more analogous to ancient Western civilisation, at least in terms of how their culture manifested itself in space.

It is not just the temples and cities that defined the landscape of the ancient world. Agriculture, and the infrastructure required to move food from the countryside to the city also had a profound impact on the land.

EASTERN CULTURES

There is a great unity of intent in the realisation of architecture and landscapes throughout the eastern cultures. From the form of buildings and their location within their landscape context, to the smallest sculptural or decorative details, style and form are consistent and intelligible across the continuum of scales. While world views and religions may have differed, a holistic view that encompassed building, landscape and ways of living on Earth and existing within the cosmos seems to have been held in common.

As with almost all cultures across the world, the landscape intended for human habitation is usually defined by a boundary – often a wall. The stupas at Sanchi, built by the Emperor Asoka, were some of the earliest Buddhist structures that acted as enclosures or boundaries. They were built to hold relics and consisted of mounded earth topped with a hemispheric dome. A gateway and a path around the dome would have been part of a meditative circuit.

Regardless of being a religious or secular site, there was always emphasis on movement through a space. This could be meditative or allegorical in the case of a religious site, or an expression of power, as was the sequence of spaces leading to the throne room at Persepolis, the capital city of ancient Persia.

Persepolis

The site of Persepolis, the capital city of the Persian Empire, was chosen for its strategic location. This location allowed excellent physical access to much of the empire, with views out from a defensible position.

The city itself was built to impress. It had a sequence of spaces designed to convey the strength of Persia and its emperor.

Buddhist stupa (Stupa No. 3) at Sanchi

The stupas at Sanchi are one of the earliest Buddhist religious complexes known, and one of the best preserved. They were built near the modern city of Bhopal in India by the Emperor Asoka. They are sited in an enclosure on a hill with fine views out to the plains below.

The Agora in Athens

The Agora (which translates roughly as 'marketplace') in Athens was central to Athenian public and democratic life, providing not only a market for goods, but also a place for generating ideas. Philosophers such as Socrates developed their ideas with a public audience in the Agora. Athens was not alone in possessing an agora. Wherever Greek culture blossomed, so did the agora.

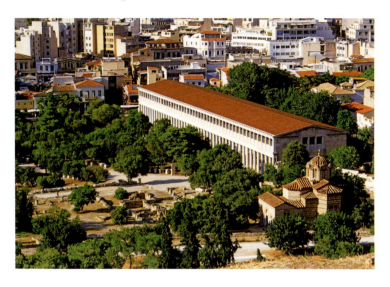

THE MEDITERRANEAN

At the heart of western civilisation is ancient Greece, which provided the foundations for science, mathematics, philosophy and politics. From Greece also came the concept of the *genius loci* – the genius or spirit of a place. At the time, this would have been a literal interpretation, a spirit or deity inhabiting a place. The same was true when the concept appeared in Rome. More importantly for the present day, it refers both to the essence of a landscape's character and to the practice of observing a place to understand where best to place built elements or plants, both for environmental reasons, such as exposure to sun, and for aesthetic reasons.

Public life in ancient Greece and Rome was of huge importance. There were places allocated for sporting events, theatre, markets and the exchange of ideas, and these were all central to the way cities were planned. The Agora was the Greek marketplace; it is analogous to our contemporary public squares, but it was much more at the heart of culture and politics. The Forum in Rome served much the same focus for Roman culture, so much so that nowadays, when we refer to a forum, we are speaking of a meeting of minds. Public space has not lost its significance for democracy and public life, and landscape architects are very much aware of its democratic function when they design for it today.

The Forum at Rome

The Roman Forum had some similarities to the Greek Agora, in that it was the centre of political and civic life. However, it lacked the underpinnings of democracy that were so crucial to the Greek state and society.

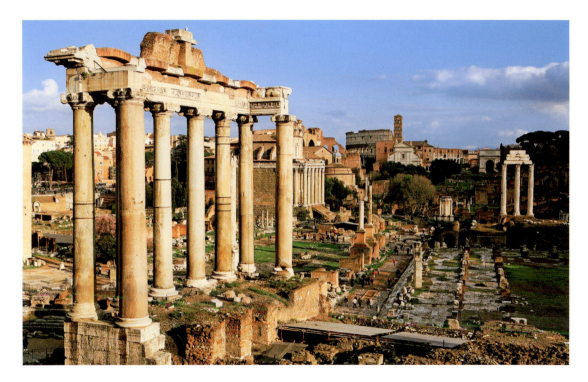

The Hippodrome at Caesarea

Public life in the ancient world also extended to great theatrical and sporting events. Chariot racing at the Hippodrome at Caesarea (in present-day Israel) would not have been so different from a visit to a racetrack today. The Hippodrome was built by Herod as part of massive building works at Caesarea.

THE MIDDLE AGES

The Middle Ages may be seen as a period of time in which superstitious religion, warring factions and authoritarian power conspired to slow the pace of progress and stifle expression. In reality, these influences did much to ensure that we have a legacy of powerful buildings and evocative landscapes that developed with strong local identities. This was not merely confined to Europe; it was also a worldwide phenomenon. Mont Saint-Michel in France, the Alhambra in Spain, the Forbidden City in Beijing and the moss garden at Saiho-ji in Kyoto were all in construction in the short space of 200 years between 1200 and 1400.

The concentration of power and money in the hands of religions, warlords and monarchs led to the construction of incredible monuments, both to the glory of a higher power and to individual vanity. Defensive structures, such as walls and castles, were also built everywhere, often providing a new defining characteristic to a landscape.

CLOISTERS AND PHYSIC GARDENS

Few, if any, great gardens were built in the Middle Ages. In the West, the tradition of growing plants outside of agriculture was confined by walls or contained within the small interior spaces of buildings (cloisters, in particular), where herbaria or physic gardens would be built. These provided herbs for cooking, perfumes and potpourris, but more importantly, for medicinal purposes. While plants and herbs may have been grown for their beauty, it is more likely that they were grown primarily for their usefulness. These, along with vegetable gardens, would have been the most formal gardens constructed.

LAND AND FEUDALISM

The control of land in the Middle Ages was highly centralised; in Europe, feudalism defined the way the landscape was subdivided and used. The bulk of the land was in the control of kings or nobles, who would use the labour of peasants to reap its benefits.

While some common land existed, it was not quite public space in the way we see it today. Common land was used for the grazing of animals and for foraging. Peasants were tied to the land so common land was therefore not symbolic of freedom and community in the way it is today.

The enclosure of lands for private ownership made a permanent change in the character of the landscape, particularly in England, whose walls and hedges have come to form a patchwork that is symbolic of the countryside and emblematic of the national temperament.

The cloister at Mont Saint-Michel, Normandy, France
Both physic gardens and cloisters were enclosed spaces. In the case of mediaeval cloisters, they were used for meditative perambulation, and would probably have provided a very welcome break from the close interiors that monks or nuns would have found themselves confined to much of the time.

Plan of Siena
A mediaeval city plan is observed
in Siena. Streets and houses were
packed tight behind defensive walls.
The public square, called the Campo
in Siena, would have provided much
of the pubic life for the community
and nearly all its pageantry.

MEDIAEVAL TOWNS

Many forces come together simultaneously to
form a town. A pleasant and productive locale,
proximity to main routes or a crossroads, a river
or a natural harbour are all good reasons for
the founding of a town. The defining elements
of settlements in the Middle Ages were
markets – seats of earthly and spiritual power
and fortifications. Productive land was highly
contested and sought after. This led to dense
settlements that occupied as little land as
possible, and to fortifications that protected the
citizenry, and more importantly, the land.

The high density led to the narrow streets and
tightly packed buildings that are characteristic
of mediaeval towns. Necessity created
environments that people find comfortable even
today; these places were built at a scale that
does not overwhelm the individual.

Although mediaeval towns, like modern towns,
would have many centres, a focus of civic power
would have developed. This public square would
have been the site of festivals and markets,
which would certainly also fall under the
watchful eye of the church or the local gentry.

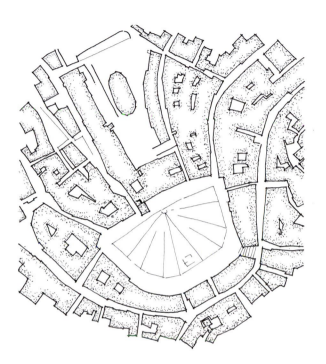

The Fundamentals of Landscape Architecture

THE RENAISSANCE AND BAROQUE

If the Middle Ages had been characterised by the claustrophobia of superstitious religion, then the Renaissance was quite the opposite. Humanism, the intellectual movement of the time, focused on people. Universities began to spring up instead of monasteries, and a quest for excellence in the arts and sciences looked to classical Greece and Rome for inspiration. Human perfection as an ideal began to be reflected in landscapes that imposed a grand geometric order upon the land.

Cities, gardens and buildings all began to reflect the ideals of perfect proportion, order and geometry. Later, the baroque period would bring more romance and fantasy to the rigidity of the spaces created in the early Renaissance, appearing in a multitude of grottos and ruined follies. Isola Bella on Lake Maggiore in Italy was an island pleasure palace designed to appear like a giant ship sailing across the lake. Its design was inspired by the same drive for fantasy that would much later create such improbable landscapes as Disneyland.

AN AWAKENING OF CREATIVITY

While life for the average person was probably not much different from the picture of grinding poverty that had been their lot for much of human history, the life of the privileged became very refined, with plenty of time for indulgence and a new spirit of playfulness.

Formal gardens became places of entertainment rather than utility, and immense effort and skill were put into their creation. Water jokes were a common feature of Renaissance and baroque gardens. These were fountains that would, for example, douse a person who stepped on a certain paving stone or a seat that would provide a damp surprise. Elaborate hydraulic systems were required for these jokes and fountains, and most were operated by gravity and not by pumps.

These periods of ostentatious materialism and display were a remarkable period for urban design as well. Places such as Bernini's Piazza del Popolo in Rome and Venice are the embodiment of baroque masterpieces.

The Royal Table at Hellbrunn

The palace at Hellbrunn, near Salzburg in Austria, has a remarkable formal garden that emphasises theatre and entertainment. Its elaborate hydraulic system powers an array of fountains as well as a water-driven mechanical theatre. 'Water jokes' were also popular in the Renaissance, and at Hellbrunn the diners at the Royal Table would be surprised by becoming part of a fountain during their meal.

The gardens of the Villa Lante, Bagnaia, Italy
Elaborate gravity-fed water features and extensive formal gardens may also be found at the Villa Lante, as at Hellbrunn. The Villa Lante is unique because the main house has been divided into two smaller houses in a very extreme bow to absolute symmetry.

FRANCE AND ITALY

The landscapes of the Renaissance reached their heights in Italy and France. The gardens at the Château de Chenonceau and André Le Nôtre's magnificent displays of wealth and power at Vaux-le-Vicomte and Louis XIV's Versailles are France's most notable contributions. The relationships between land, water, sky and geometry were all extremely studied, deliberate and used to create vast pleasure grounds. The contrast between intellectual pursuit and frivolity can often be seen in the gardens of the Renaissance.

Italy is home to a profusion of exuberant formal gardens, and though no one designer quite stands as head and shoulders above the crowd as Le Nôtre, there was a strong tradition of styles and forms that found unique expressions in each and every landscape. As in France, water and geometry provided a strong framework for the gardens, but the regions of Italy around Rome, Florence and Tuscany, where many of these gardens may be found, were blessed with more dramatic topography. Many Italian baroque gardens are composed of series of terraces stepping down, which allow for the water to be animated in fountains at each step. Ingenious and beautiful devices for transporting water were employed, and many fountains were remarkable displays, in particular, the Water Organ at the Villa d'Este at Tivoli.

View of the gardens at Vaux-le-Vicomte, France

While Versailles is his most elaborate garden, Vaux-le-Vicomte is arguably André Le Nôtre's masterpiece. As a composition, it was intended to be viewed from the château, but it also provides an ideal formal setting for the palace.

ANDRÉ LE NÔTRE

André Le Nôtre grew up in a family of gardeners where he gained experience in methods of garden design, plants and planting in some of the most celebrated parks and gardens of the age. He was gifted in painting and studied architecture for several years. As an adult, he took on gardening duties for King Louis XIV.

Le Nôtre's first large garden was one of the masterpieces of the Baroque period at Vaux-le-Vicomte. Nicolas Fouquet, the owner of the château, was in charge of finances for the court of Louis XIV. Fouquet was imprisoned after the opulence of the garden confirmed the King's suspicions that he was lining his pockets from the government's coffers.

Louis XIV was determined to outdo Fouquet's garden, hiring Le Nôtre to lay out the gardens at the Palace of Versailles. Le Nôtre created many remarkable gardens through his career, but the perfection in the geometry, views and perspectives of Versailles and Vaux-le-Vicomte will always be his crowning glory.

THE ENGLISH LANDSCAPE

While Italy and France were clearly dominant in the creation of great gardens through the sixteenth and seventeenth centuries, the geometric style was well exercised in many other European countries, not least in the Netherlands and Spain. England, too, much under the influence of France during this period, saw the building of Hampton Court amongst a number of other formal gardens. Sir Christopher Wren's unrealised plan for the City of London after the Great Fire in 1666 is also a classic baroque city plan.

The rolling hills of the English landscape called for a different and more indigenous treatment. The eighteenth century saw the stirrings of interest in the natural environment and a romanticisation of the countryside, including the forbidding mountains and deep forests, which had previously been seen as wastelands to be avoided.

This interest in the picturesque led to the creation of landscapes composed of exquisite views, rolling lawns, pools and groupings of trees that mirrored the landscape paintings being created at the time. Champions for this type of landscape were architects such as William Kent, Charles Bridgeman, and most famously, Capability Brown. This revolutionary style was to have a global influence on landscape design, as the style for parks that is still predominant, and as the foundation for modern landscape architecture.

LANCELOT 'CAPABILITY' BROWN

Lancelot Brown became known as Capability Brown for his habit of pointing out the 'capabilities' of the landscapes to his clients for which he intended to design, often referring to the *genius loci*.

Brown was a prolific English landscape architect who lived from 1716 to 1783. Along with his contemporaries, William Kent and Charles Bridgeman, he created the English style of landscape that was, for the time, distinctively informal, creating a pastoral, picturesque setting. Among his masterpieces are the gardens at Blenheim Palace, Warwick Castle and Croome Court.

The grounds at Blenheim Palace
This was one of Capability Brown's most influential landscapes, and is absolutely characteristic of the style of the English School of Landscape Design. The house, rather than being framed by a formal garden, is instead placed in a picturesque, pastoral setting with a large, placid lake and rolling lawns that come right up to the door. The park's design was tremendously influential both in England and internationally.

**The Stroll Garden at Katsura
Imperial Palace, Kyoto, Japan**
A Japanese stroll garden, also called
a tour garden, was designed for
walking. At Katsura, the path is a
loop around a central lake, and there
are possibilities for exploration off
the main path. The garden must
be experienced in motion and as
a sequence.

THE EAST

It is a challenge to place the landscapes of the
East on the same timeline as those of the West,
as the intellectual and philosophical influences
(and their timings) upon them were different.
However, the interaction between East and
West, made possible by great leaps forward
in technology, transportation and navigation,
created certain parallels in the landscape as
images and ideas were exchanged.

The Mughal gardens of India, such as
Shalimar Bagh and Nishat Bagh, showed formal
symmetries and geometries based upon an
ideal of heavenly paradise (the word 'paradise'
was originally a synonym for 'garden'). These
gardens predated the rational symmetries of
the Renaissance. In China, the Summer Palaces
of Beijing were designed for short walking
journeys through a microcosm of nature.
Every stone and tree had symbolic significance.
Japan had its 'stroll gardens', also known as
paradise gardens, which were intended for
exploration on foot, and where each element
was of profound importance.

THE NINETEENTH CENTURY

Three revolutions marked the beginning of the nineteenth century, fundamentally changing both the political and the physical landscape of the world. The American Revolution established the United States as an ambitious, independent, democratic power and shortly afterwards, France shrugged off the yoke of monarchy. The end of the 1700s also marked the beginning of the Industrial Revolution. Europe – Britain, in particular – and the USA were the great powers of the nineteenth century. As a result, the changes in attitudes towards the landscape were influenced mostly by these regions.

The great drive towards urbanisation that continues to the present day picked up pace. The inequalities between rich and poor were made all the more stark by overcrowded, polluted and squalid urban conditions, which were made a reality by the centralisation of industry. Among other factors, this helped bring about a rise in philanthropic thought and action. One response was the creation of public parks in order to offer relief and escape from the stark urban reality. Many of these parks were not just for the wealthy; they also offered their charms to the masses. New York's Central Park is a shining example of this public generosity.

This period was an amazing time for cities in other ways, too. Paris, which at the beginning of the 1800s was still in essence a mediaeval city, was pierced through with the broad boulevards that now define it. In London, Regent Street was joined with The Regent's Park in a single, united piece of urban theatre.

EUROPE

A spirit of romance and fantasy, together with hard-headed technological advances, allowed for the creation of the most memorable landscapes in Europe, with most of them being urban. In Paris, Baron Georges-Eugène Haussmann led a massive urban regeneration programme that involved driving huge boulevards through the city's congested core, bringing in light, air and modern amenities such as sewers. Haussmann often worked with JC Alphand, an engineer with a keen eye for landscape. Alphand was a model, in fact, of the present-day landscape architect – comfortable with urbanism, with a flair for engineering and an eye for beauty.

Streets and public parks were central to public life and the modern profession of landscape architecture began to find its voice in this environment. The Englischer Garten (English Garden) in Munich is a vast public park that predated New York's Central Park, and survives today as a vibrant amenity for the city. Barcelona was graced with the Eixample district and Gaudí's fantastical Parc Güell was constructed.

JC Alphand's Parc des Buttes-Chaumont, Paris, France, 1863
An early example of adaptive reuse, the Parc des Buttes-Chaumont was built in an abandoned quarry. The dramatic topography created by the stone quarry creates a park with a real air of fantasy. It was furnished in a naturalistic style, with curving pathways and rustic, romantic features.

THE BRITISH ISLES

The British Isles, sitting as it did at the helm of a substantial empire and driving a massive industrial machine, enriched and embellished its landscape in accordance with its wealth. However, the Industrial Revolution swallowed up whole areas of the country into industrial grime, as dire and foul as some areas were fair and lovely. The railways brought explosive growth into the countryside and allowed suburbanisation to occur. As in the rest of Europe, the drive to create, build and engineer was paired with a propensity for flights of the imagination.

John Nash's plan for west London was a vast architectural set piece that stretched from St James's Park in the south and up Regent Street, through Piccadilly Circus and Oxford Circus, before terminating with grand effect in The Regent's Park. A bit short of public-friendly, it was intended to separate prosperous Mayfair from down-at-heel Soho. More public-minded projects were greatly influential. The Crystal Palace for the Great Exhibition of 1851 was set in extensive grounds and Birkenhead Park in Liverpool was built as an amenity for rich and poor alike.

THE UNITED STATES

Phenomenal growth from the period around 1800 to the turn of the next century left much of North America utterly transformed, and in this time, America grew into a world power. Initially, the resources of a vast continent looked limitless, and roads and railways snaked out across the land to build a new type of empire. A sense of collective ownership of the landscape meant that the marks of occupation were not as clear in the US as they were in Europe. Private gardens merged together to create seamless parklands. Americans thus came to regard their wild hinterlands as part of a continuum that began at home.

This public spirit was to find real resonance within the emerging profession of landscape architecture, particularly through the voice of one man – Frederick Law Olmsted. Olmsted had travelled widely in the US and Europe, and had been an enlightened farmer in New England. On his travels, he was much impressed by Liverpool's Birkenhead Park. He based his design for New York's Central Park on the public spirit he had witnessed in Liverpool.

Olmsted was a man of many talents, skilled at drawing many diverse influences into brilliant designs. He understood that the landscape is composed of many different layers ranging from environment and ecology, to the social and political, through to the rural and the urban. He designed not just parks and gardens, but suburban neighbourhoods, park systems, and even what might have amounted to the first sustainable drainage system at Boston's Back Bay.

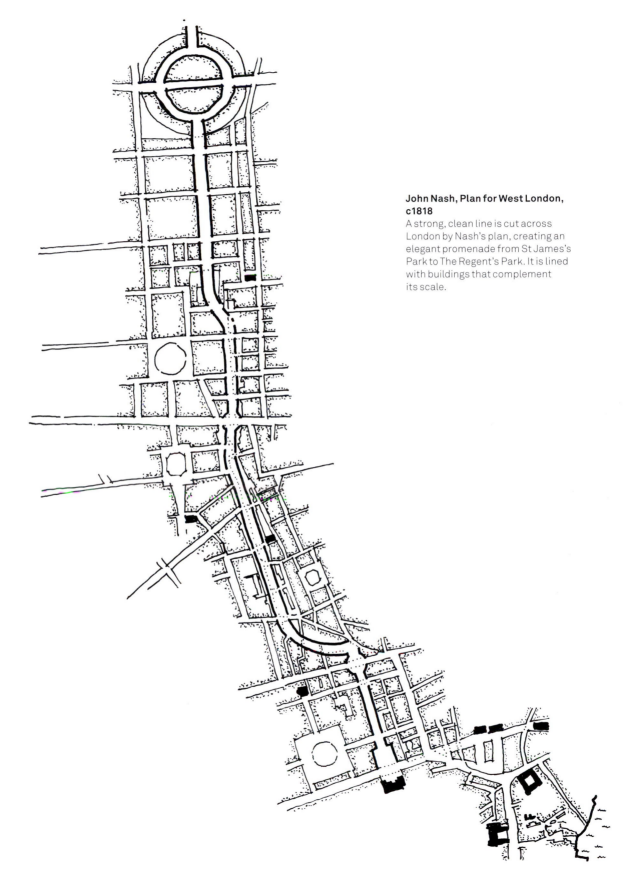

John Nash, Plan for West London, c1818

A strong, clean line is cut across London by Nash's plan, creating an elegant promenade from St James's Park to The Regent's Park. It is lined with buildings that complement its scale.

THE TWENTIETH CENTURY

Human history has never known a more turbulent and energetic century than the last one. The machine that was the Industrial Revolution, once set in motion, launched progress full tilt at its outset, and the speed of change remained constant until its end. The gains in technology, science and medicine were matched by destruction in horrific wars and by pollution. Humanity used technology to conquer every stretch of the landscape.

Landscape architecture came of age in this period, building upon the creative legacy of individuals, such as Olmsted, in order to become a profession based in a truly holistic view of landscape. New methods for analysing the landscape, separating information such as soils, vegetation and demographics into layers, were developed by the path-breaking American landscape architect, Ian McHarg. His seminal book, *Design with Nature* (1969), set out the principles of this approach. It was revolutionary for landscape planning and design, which led to the development of Geographic Information Systems (GIS).

The creation of vast national parks, garden cities, picturesque highways, and the need for large-scale land planning, created many opportunities for landscape architects. Working with scales much beyond the private garden began to underline divisions within the profession – between garden and landscape designers, urbanists and landscape planners.

The predominant architectural style throughout the century was Modernism, which emphasised purity of form and the importance of function, casting aside the frippery of ornament and attempting to build a new aesthetic that purported to be unencumbered by historical reference. Early modernists cherished the belief that good design could make a great positive difference to the lives of ordinary people.

MODERNIST GARDENS

Both public and private modernist gardens were realised with the same aim for purity of form and function – the chief trait of modernist design in general. A crisis of confidence was encountered when designers were faced with the reality that many, if not all, plants must be regarded as ornamental. For garden designers, this often meant a rejection of a standard palette of plants in favour of more formal 'architectural' plants. It also entailed the adoption of quite rigid forms in the overall structure of gardens.

Biomorphic (organic) forms that appeared vividly in the work of artists, in particular the paintings and sculptures of Jean Arp, also gave some relief from rectilinear forms in gardens.

Since the early days of Modernism, though, designers have become more relaxed about having to conform to such high standards of intellectual purity, and have opened themselves up to a broader range of influences.

Thomas Church, Donnell Garden, California, 1948
The Donnell Garden was the very picture of modern living, with its serene biomorphic pool, which is not only a pool but also a plinth for an abstract sculpture. The California style that the Donnell Garden became emblematic of was all about living outdoors. The garden was never intended as a setting for architecture, but as a living space all its own.

THE MODERN CITY

Cities were made and remade with dizzying speed throughout the twentieth century, and their expression reflected different values and political systems. Dictators and authoritarian governments sought to glorify themselves and their regimes through massive programmes of demolition and building. Hitler, Stalin, Mussolini and Mao Zedong all built forbidding and inhuman urban landscapes that sought to express the omniscience of an all-powerful state. More recently, despots such as Nicolae Ceaçescu in Romania and Saddam Hussein in Iraq tried to accomplish much the same with their own capital cities. However, a humanist, socialist model of city building was much in evidence in this period as well.

The garden city movement initiated by Ebenezer Howard with his book *Garden Cities of To-morrow* (1902) sought to create commodious communities outside city centres, complete with their own transportation systems of canals, road and rail. Welwyn Garden City in England is another example, as is the town of Radburn, New Jersey. Radburn is remarkable for its careful separation of cars and pedestrians, and by the park landscape into which the homes are integrated. Many of these concepts were revisited in another English garden city – Milton Keynes.

In great cities, there has been a constant struggle between two factions. One side believes cities can be conceived and constructed as a mass, while the other camp holds the view that cities must be allowed to grow slowly and incrementally, so that a community might be nurtured within a town that grows to accommodate it over time. Jane Jacobs was a great proponent of the latter view, and her book, *The Death and Life of Great American Cities* (1961), has proven itself as a handbook for urban designers and planners.

Brasilia, Brazil, 1957–1961

Brasilia was built as a new capital for a forward-looking Brazil. It is located at the heart of the country, unlike Brazil's first capital, Rio de Janeiro, which was located at the coastal periphery. The plan was built with lightning speed, taking only four years to be designed and built. The city took the form of an aeroplane or bird, and was strictly zoned into separate functions. In a way, it was as much a sculpture as a city.

POSTMODERNISM

Modernism was bound to provoke a reaction, as its puritanical insistence on unembellished form was viewed as a straitjacket by some designers. Postmodernism was an often chaotic return to influence, and designers liberally referenced other visual cues from virtually any historic period or style. Postmodern design was at its height in the 1980s and 1990s, a time when exuberant corporate growth was creating a desire for display rather than for the restrained architectural forms of Modernism.

Postmodern design was strongly tied to currents of thought in literary theory, such as deconstructionism and structuralism. The influence of these movements on all the arts was marked through this period, and has yet to run its course. At present, tensions still arise between designers who support Modernism and those who uphold postmodernist values.

Charles Moore, Piazza d'Italia, 1978
In Postmodernism, a return to the use of ornament and to the architectural forms of the past was seen as a way to communicate identity and create place. Moore's Piazza d'Italia is a prime example of how postmodern design combined exaggerated or stereotypical elements together to create a sense of hyperrealism that flirted with kitsch.

Bernard Tschumi, Parc de la Villette, Paris, 1987–1991
The designs for the Parc de la Villette were a complex layering of theory, programme and geometry. The park combines the formal qualities of the French baroque with more contemporary ideas drawn from the practice of montage in cinema, among other concepts. Bright red 'follies' are distributed around the park on a grid. The grid is then sliced through with strong diagonals and traversed by snaking pathways and plants.

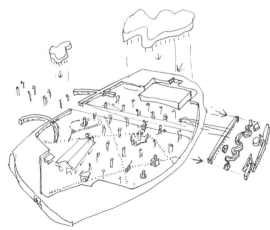

MILLENNIAL LANDSCAPES

Landscape architecture, having defined itself through the course of the twentieth century, faces a new challenge – that of coming to maturity and taking its place as the profession most suited to guiding development in a century where it will become more and more of an imperative to develop in harmony with the natural functions of the planet. We can now see that present economies based upon the myth of limitless growth are untenable, and landscape architecture is one of the few professions with a broad enough view to suggest sustainable alternatives.

Postmodernism gave designers the option to freely quote other periods and styles, thus giving landscape architecture an impressive range to respond to a larger context. This artistic and stylistic range sits comfortably with the broad scope of landscape architecture in general.

West 8, Schouwburgplein, Rotterdam, 1996
Construction of the Schouwburgplein in Rotterdam was severely limited by the existence of a parking garage directly below the site. Lightweight decking was used to provide visual texture and interest to the project. The expanse of decking forms a stage for human activity. To add to the kinetic activity and interest of the site, a set of four mechanical lights randomly move like swans' necks above the square. These echo the forms of the cranes on Rotterdam's waterfront.

2

SITE AND CONTEXT

When a word or phrase is taken out of context, it can become meaningless, or worse, its meaning can become distorted, even to the point of saying the opposite of what was originally intended. This is why journalists are often heard to say 'context is everything'.

Context is no less important in the landscape. The landscape provides context for everything that is built and for the activities of our daily lives. Anything that is built in the landscape needs to take into account its surroundings and its situation to be successful and sustainable – and this work is at the core of the practice of landscape architecture.

Margie Ruddick, Study for Estuaries Center, New York
This study sited a conceptual plan for a centre for the study of rivers and estuaries in New York State. The design is a careful dialogue between land, water, buildings and scientific study.

LANDSCAPE: SITE AND CONTEXT

'The city, the suburbs, and the countryside must be viewed as a single, evolving system with nature, as must every individual park and building within that larger whole.'
Anne Whiston Spirn

Everything in the landscape is part of an interconnected system that makes up the fabric of our existence. In order to understand the landscape and its workings, it is necessary to learn to look at all aspects contextually, to think and act holistically. It is common to refer to the exterior or urban environment as a fabric, and this metaphor is born of the realisation that if any one element in the landscape is altered, everything else is affected as well – much in the same way that tugging on a single thread can unravel a scarf. Indeed, sometimes, a bit of a pull on a single thread is all that's required to tighten up and finish a fabric.

Landscape architecture is an inexact field. When there are so many elements to work with, we come up against the limits of human ability. With humility and the best of intentions, the landscape architect seeks to put everything in order, in context, so that all the various human and natural functions that are required of a landscape are accommodated.

WHAT IS A SITE?

Many people will have rarely heard the term 'site' by itself, but rather accompanied by another modifying term, such as 'building site' or 'website'. In both cases, the term refers to an area (physical, in the case of building, and virtual on the web) that has been marked out with the intention that action will occur there, that there will be a human use for that spot. It takes very little to mark a site. A simple staff, thrust into the ground, changes in its function from a walking stick to a landmark. It becomes the marker of a claim on that space of earth and all that is visible from it. The landscape around it swims into focus. It now has human meaning and is the context for a site. The first step has been made in creating a place.

Mary Miss, Field Rotation, Illinois, USA
An open field near Governor State is the site for Mary Miss's sculptural landscape installation from 1981. A central pit anchors the work in the landscape, and a series of posts spiral out from the centre as though flung out by centrifugal force. The exposed and elemental character of the work shows, in an almost primitive way, what it means to mark out a place on the earth. The urge to inhabit space by marking it is a fundamentally human one .

SITE INVENTORY AND ANALYSIS

When a landscape architect is given a job to do, it almost always involves a specific site, and since there is no such thing as a completely blank site where anything is possible, the first thing to do is to come to grips with the character and qualities of the place.

Site inventory is just as it sounds. It is a list – an account of everything that exists on a site. This establishes the context in which the designer will work. The inventory includes all the aspects that define a place. It is important to know the history of a site – from the formation of the land, to its human inhabitation and use. A list is made of the vegetation to be found on the site. Social and economic elements are examined, such as whether the site is in a poor area or a wealthy suburb. Geology, soils and the flow of water across a site are important. Prevailing winds are noted, exposure to sun is charted. It is usually necessary to spend a great deal of time actually on the site in order to compile an inventory. All this comes together into a profile of the site that the designer can then begin to approach and question. Finally, the designer's first impressions and emotional, subjective response to the site must be carefully balanced with the facts.

Site analysis is the process of finding the implications to the characteristics that are listed in the inventory. If a site is on a slope facing away from the sun and in temperate environments, it is likely to be inhospitable, especially in winter. This can have profound implications on whether or not it is appropriate to build on a given site. If a site is liable to flooding, it is highly inadvisable to build underground car parking.

Analysis is often greatly aided by different drawing techniques. These allow the designer to compare and contrast the different elements of the site inventory. Layering site information in the manner developed by Ian McHarg, which is greatly aided by Geographic Information Systems (GIS) and other computer imaging, is vital to contemporary practice.

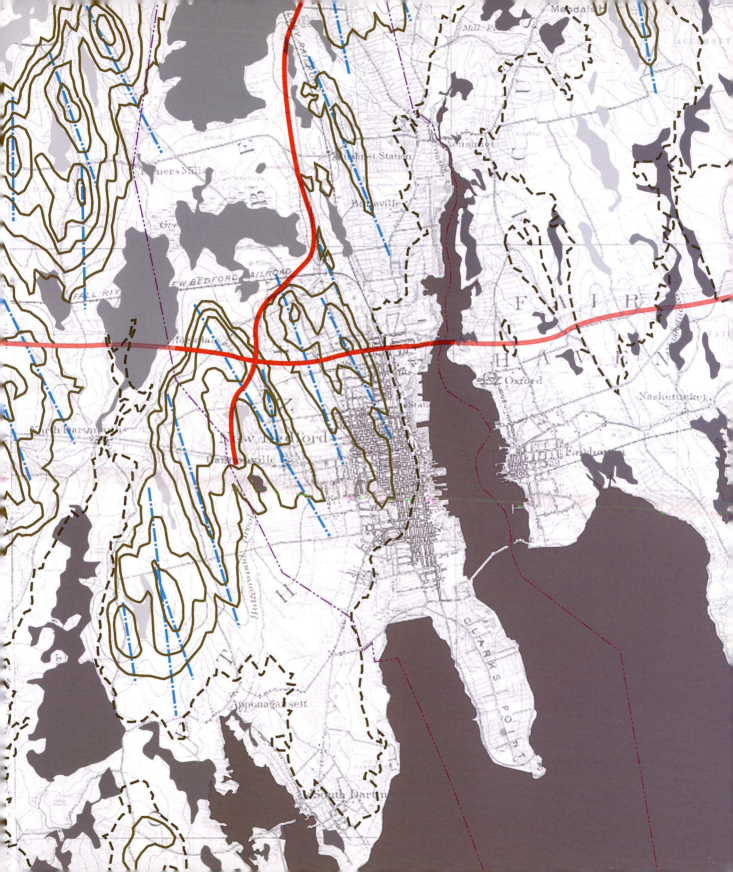

Recording the site on video
These images helped StoSS Landscape Urbanism develop their masterplan for highway corridors in New Bedford. Video is not just useful for high-speed sequences like this, but also to capture the ever-shifting sights and sounds of a site, including the movement of people, the lapping of water and the changes in light.

RECORDING THE SITE

The twentieth-century American landscape architect AE Bye worked primarily on site. He spent hours and days simply watching the moods of a landscape, seeking to understand its daily and seasonal rhythms. His zen-like methods produced the gardens for the Soros estate on Long Island in New York, where carefully placed mounds capture snow on their shady sides – patterns that Bye intended. Most busy landscape architects do not have the luxury to spend quite so much time on each site nowadays, and thus, we tend to rely much more on technology.

Digital imagery provides much of the site documentation that landscape architects rely upon to create their designs. Photography at the ground level is of primary importance, allowing an understanding of the human experience of the landscape at the scale of walking. Aerial photography, shot from planes or satellite, reveals detail that might be unseen at ground level. Video, as well, may offer more than any other medium. Landscapes are constantly in motion, and video allows us to document the site in real time and in a way that is most like the human experience of a place.

One of the most important tools for recording the site is the hand sketch. It is a true representation of what people actually see.

MAPPING THE SITE

Mapping is a key element of both site inventory and the analysis and design process. In combination with sketches, photographs and video, mapping helps us to complete the picture of a site. A sketch of a river, for example, might not be of any assistance in ascertaining in which direction it flows. A specific mapping of the flow of water through an area, using arrows to show the direction of flow, can convey a great deal of information about a site. Further, the river sketch can be marked on the map, along with the direction the artist was looking while making the sketch. Mapping and recording then combine to build a clear picture of the site that others can understand, even if they have never visited the place themselves.

Mapping shows not only what exists, but also what possibilities exist. They offer a way of testing different possibilities for design.

Physical site characteristics are first and foremost in the landscape architect's mind throughout the process of design, and the remainder of this chapter explores the basic categories that are encountered on any site. These variables will be mapped, recorded and considered to form the foundation for the design process.

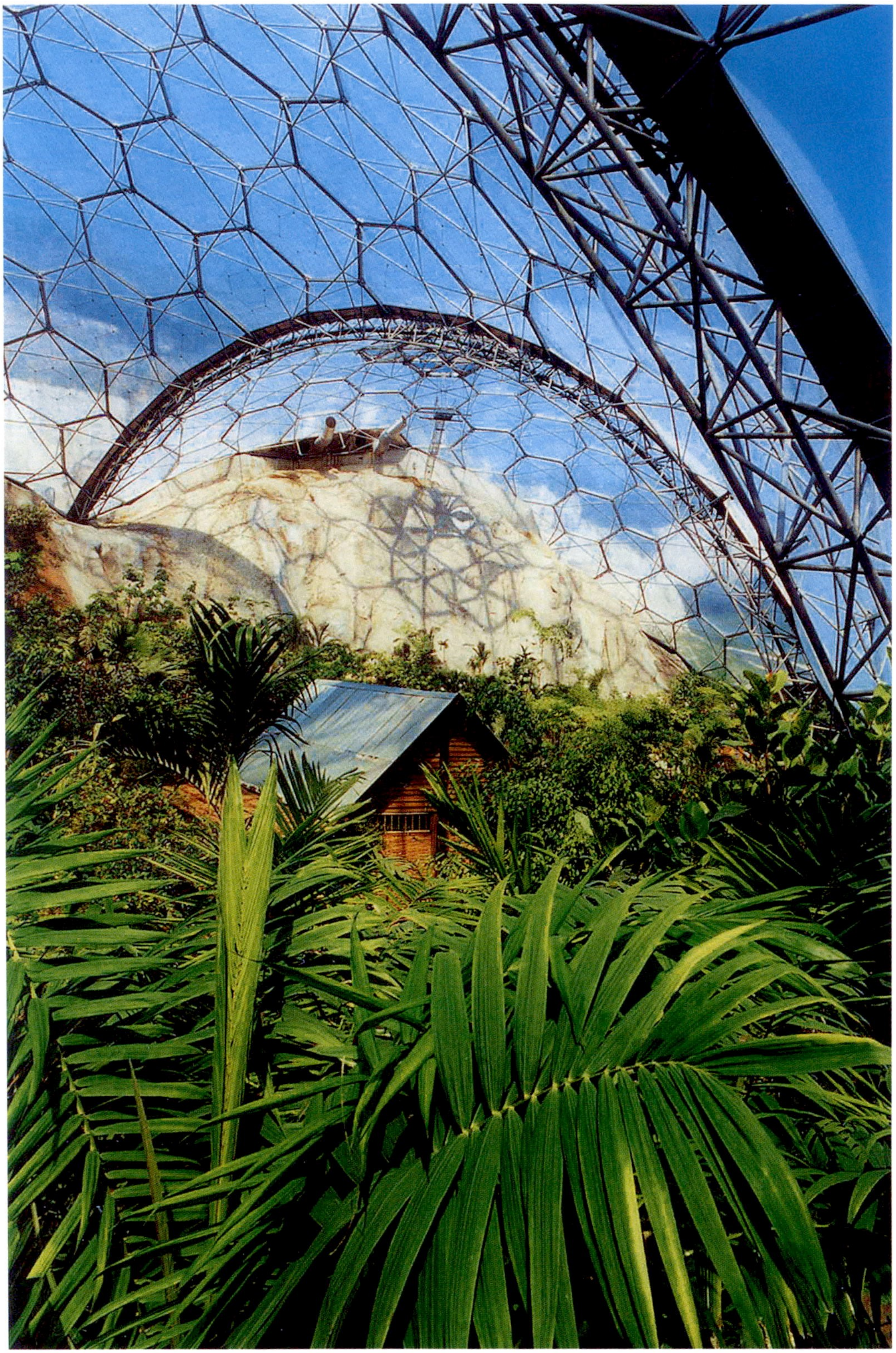

CLIMATE

Weather is the atmospheric conditions occurring outside your window right now, and what might be forecast for the rest of the week. Climate is composed of the larger weather trends or averages that affect an area on a more general basis; whether an area is hot and dry, or mild and damp, for example. The largest trends in climate are determined remotely. Climate patterns stem from the earth's proximity to the sun's heat in its elliptical orbit, and the angle of the inclination of its axis. On the surface of the globe, the temperature differential between the poles and the equator, again a result of the sun's energy, cause thermal air and water currents that spread the sun's heat around the planet. These currents are strong determining factors for weather patterns.

Local climate patterns are determined by a great range of variables. Temperatures become cooler the higher the elevation above sea level. Clouds can pile up against a mountain range along a coast, and water evaporated from the ocean will be wrung out of them. A great expanse of desert will superheat in the daytime under cloudless, moistureless skies, but temperatures will plunge at night without the insulation that clouds provide.

CLIMATES AND REGIONS

There are four very broadly defined climatic regions of the globe. These are: cold, cool-temperate, warm-humid and hot-dry regions. Each of these have distinct types of vegetation and topography. The kinds of human activities that take place in these four regions are all very different as well. The most variable conditions are in the cool-temperate region, where there is a marked difference in the seasons.

Biomes at the Eden Project, Cornwall, UK

A biome is the total ecology associated with a given climate region. The Eden Project recreates two primary biomes of Earth under giant domes for the benefit of comparative study, and for the simple pleasure of interaction. The humid tropics and the warm temperate regions are represented, allowing a range of plants to survive, which would not otherwise endure Britain's winters. Naturally, it is much more difficult to recreate the conditions in the cold regions without elaborate and expensive air conditioning.

University Square, Tromsø, Norway
In the extreme north, seasonal changes in vegetation may not be as pronounced, but landscapes may still register changing conditions dramatically. At University Square in Tromsø, a placid fountain sits at the centre of an elegant spiral. Early in the year, the water reflects back the freshness of spring. As the winter sets in, the small variations in topography are thrown into high relief by snow, shadow and the long light. The long Arctic winter requires that landscapes are responsive at night time, and lighting can transform a space.

THE SEASONS

In cool-temperate regions, the seasons animate landscapes throughout the year. The rhythms and patterns of daily life change slowly from one season to the next, giving life a pleasing texture and variety.

Spring is the season for awakening from winter, planting and watching new growth occur. The first flowers of spring are a sight for sore eyes, and people eagerly anticipate these harbingers of better weather and fresh food. In summer, days are long and productive, while in autumn, the days begin to cool and shorten. In some places the leaves of deciduous trees provide colourful displays. Finally, winter, with its short days and cold weather, keeps us indoors and dreaming of spring.

The seasons make planting choices exciting, with something new to look forward to in each season. Some plants give full measure in every season. For example, *Cornus florida* – the flowering dogwood – provides elegant flowers in spring; refined leaves and colourful berries through summer; striking leaf colour in autumn; and a sculptural shape to the trunks and attractive bark on trees during winter.

A microclimate at the Isabella Plantation in Richmond Park, London
Sheltered from winds by dense plantings, shaded, and cooled by a pond, this shamelessly pretty spot in Richmond Park is a favourite for lovers and picnickers.

MICROCLIMATES

The patterns in which we use everyday spaces, such as urban squares and gardens, are shaped largely by microclimates. Again, climate in this sense refers to an average of conditions on a given site, but in this case to a very specific location. In the northern hemisphere, for example, the northern face of an east–west wall will be cold and shaded, while the south face will be a warm, sunny pocket. This is important for planting choices and affects the way people use a space. In winter, a square with little shade might be an attraction on sunny days. However, it would be a pitilessly exposed place in summer, which would attract few people.

Design can do little to change climate, but microclimates may be manipulated very effectively on the smallest of sites. Extremes can be moderated by the provision of windbreaks or by channelling cooling breezes. Water in any form can have a cooling effect in an urban space. Plants also have a strong influence on microclimates, providing shade, moisture and protection from wind. Every place has a different mix and the manipulation of microclimates makes for stimulating design work.

CLIMATE CHANGE

Climate change has been much in the news lately and its effects are beginning to make themselves felt in weather patterns, in crop yields, and in the relative comfort of outdoor spaces. The current trend is towards an average warming of global temperatures that is melting polar ice and increasing the intensity of storms around the world. We can only make educated guesses about the long-term effects of climate change, and predictions range from the merely uncomfortable to the dire and catastrophic.

Landscape architects have an important part to play in adapting to climate change as it is a crisis taking place in the landscape. Climate change will have local impacts on water systems, weather, temperatures and on animal and plant species. All of this will require the expertise of a holistic, problem-solving profession, and landscape architecture quite neatly fits the bill.

Dongtan Eco-city, China

Dongtan is a completely planned community on an island in the estuary of the Yangtze River. The community is designed to be largely self-sufficient, producing its own power from a variety of sources, including waste. Public transportation is a priority, as well as providing for bicycle and pedestrian traffic. Some food will be provided from nearby farms. New developments of this sort can provide a solid model for how we might adapt existing communities to combat climate change. Landscape architects can play a very central role in adapting and retrofitting the existing built environment.

LAND

The importance of land can be measured by the amount of fighting we do over it. From the simple disputes of neighbours to all-out war, the control over land and the drawing and redrawing of boundaries has been a hallmark of the exercise of power throughout history. This is not merely because the possession of land is symbolic, but because of everything land has to offer. Land is a resource that provides us with food, habitat, building materials and fuel. It provides both work and recreation – those activities that give meaning to our lives.

A number of important intangibles are provided by the land as well – a sense of belonging, identity, beauty, and even love. Such things may sound sentimental, but they are basic to human nature, and it is a truism to say that emotions often gain the upper hand on reason. Greed, unfortunately, often overwhelms all, and as a result we have squandered our resources in the pursuit of a very one-dimensional type of profit. It is up to professions such as landscape architecture to begin pointing the way back to the values based in the land that represent real profit, in all its dimensions.

Landscape architects are stewards of the land. They learn to 'read' the land's forms and expressions and work to improve our use of the land's surface and its resources.

STONE AND SOIL

The earth's crust is formed of rock of various types, extruded, exploded, heated, squeezed, or laid down in layers of sediment. This rock is part of a dynamic planetary system that is constantly being worn down at the same time it is replaced, always striving for equilibrium, but never quite achieving it. The action of wind, water, ice and plants upon the rock breaks it up and wears it away into particles of various sizes that form the mineral base for the earth's incredibly thin, but incredibly precious, layer of soil.

Good, fertile soil is formed as plants gain a foothold in these mineral particles and begin to build up the levels of organic matter within the soil. Grassland soils can be among the most fertile, with generations of plants layered over each other and held in place by the strong roots and fine structure of the grasses. Grazing animals contribute their dung to the mix, and the result is deep and productive topsoil. However, the creation of healthy topsoil takes time. The Dust Bowl on the North American plains in the 1930s, where millions of tonnes of soil simply blew away due to poor land management and drought, provides a vivid image of just how fragile this system can be and how quickly it can all disappear.

Soil layers

The wildlife garden at the Natural History Museum in London provides a window into the layers of a heathland soil. Heathers and grasses reach their roots into a rich organic layer made up of rotted plant material, which lies atop another layer of peat. Below that, there is sandy, free-draining subsoil. All soils show layers and they are part of the key to classifying soils.

The landscape of Cappadocia in Turkey

The land we live upon shapes how we live, what we eat, our view of the world at large, and our whole identities. In the region of Cappadocia in Turkey, a geologic mix of sedimentary and volcanic rocks resulted in a bizarre and jagged landscape. Generations of Cappadocians carved their homes into the soft volcanic stone of the 'fairy chimneys'. Whole communities are carved into the rock.

LAND AND LAW

A significant portion of the law profession is occupied with the business of land law. Likewise, governments around the world are constantly under pressure to redefine land areas and land uses to satisfy the needs of, perhaps most often, major corporations (especially the agricultural giants), but also of various non-profit or pressure groups that for one reason or another have a stake in the land. There is a constant tug-of-war between those concerned with the protection and conservation of land and resources, and those who seek to exploit them. Both ends are necessary and landscape architects are often called in to help guide this process, as expert witnesses and mediators who are often sympathetic to both parties.

Land law and land use planning often go hand in hand, as each is concerned with the definition of boundaries and the definition of what activities will occur within them.

LAND USE

Land use is the human activity that takes place on a site. Often this use is exploitative, where people are extracting resources for example, forestry, mining, or agriculture. Land may be used for industry, for commerce, for transportation, or for dwelling, among many other possibilities. Some land uses have a very light touch on the planet – the use of a bird preserve for birdwatching, for example. Others have devastating impact, such as the deforestation of the Amazon basin rainforests for the production of beef and soya beans.

Land-use planning tries to balance the needs of people with the needs of the planet, ensuring that a wide variety of plants can grow in healthy soil to support a wide selection of wildlife. Every place on Earth has something to give to the overall health of the planet. There is no such thing as waste land. We place economic value on the extraction of resources from the land, but there is no accounting mechanism to subtract value when we've used something up. When an oil field is drained or when a forest becomes a desert, the value is lost forever. This may sound dire, but many landscape architects are employed just to make sure that we don't make these kinds of mistakes. It is a profession for people who want to change the world for the better, one patch of ground and one land use at a time.

The Fundamentals of Landscape Architecture

WATER

Water is constantly in motion, and the effects of this motion are visible in almost every part of our existence on the planet. Water is also fundamental to shaping the face of the Earth through erosion and the nature and character of our landscapes. Oceans, seas, lakes, rivers and streams all powerfully shape the visual and environmental qualities of a landscape. Equally, the amount of rainfall an area receives will have a profound effect on the type and quantity of vegetation to be found there.

Water has unique qualities, allowing it to appear as a clear liquid, fog, steam, or ice. In combination with the Earth's atmosphere and climates, it may be seen as rain, sleet, hail, mist, fog, snow, icicles, icebergs, glaciers and our dwindling, but still majestic, polar ice caps.

Lastly, and most obviously, water is essential to all life on the planet. It is an indispensable, but limited, resource that requires the care and maintenance of landscape architects and all.

WATER SYSTEMS

The constant motion of water creates the climate and weather systems that shape the landscape and thus the nature of life on Earth. Water falls from the sky as precipitation (rain, snow, etc). If it falls on land, it is absorbed by plants and soil or it runs off the land's surface, forming streams that become rivers, which flow to the sea. Water also evaporates from plants, soil, and the surface of water into the air, where it can once again fall as rain.

There are other types of important water systems that are of more immediate concern to landscape architects. These include systems for removing storm water from streets and pavements and systems of water transportation, such as rivers and canals. At the smallest scale, which can often still be very grand, these systems include fountains, ponds and pools in landscape and garden design.

Water is also a resource for more than merely supporting life. It can make life more pleasurable in the form of water-based recreation and water sports. It can cool the air in a city square or a garden on a hot summer day. It can provide us with beauty, scenery, along with sights and sounds that reduce stress, increase happiness and enrich our lives.

Living Water Park, Chengdu, Sichuan, China

The landscape architect Margie Ruddick created Living Water Park for Chengdu. The park works with water on many levels, cleaning pollutants from it while allowing people to interact with the water and to provide recreation and enjoyment.

The park demonstrates the cleansing of water through biological methods and serves as a model for safe and thoughtful practice in China and throughout the world.

Water Pollution Control Laboratory, Portland, Oregon, USA

The city of Portland, Oregon, has been at the forefront of using sustainable drainage in a great variety of applications and types of area. Murase Associates, a landscape architecture firm renowned for its imaginative and progressive work with water, created the Water Pollution Control Laboratory for the City of Portland as an experimental installation in treating large volumes of storm water. The laboratory is a landscape that is both useful and functional. Instead of being hidden away in a sewer, the water is made part of a visible celebration.

SUSTAINABLE DRAINAGE SYSTEMS

Sustainable drainage refers to the safe and effective management of rainwater and surface water, collectively known as storm water. This is known in the UK and Europe as Sustainable Drainage Systems (SuDS) and in the USA as Best Management Practice (BMP).

While 'drainage' might sound like an unpleasant activity, it is actually a process that requires understanding of many related natural systems, which is exciting not just for the beautiful and useful landscapes that can result, but for the promise it has to improve the environment for people and animals.

Many of our most serious floods are the result of surface water from torrential rain. These floods are made more serious by the large impermeable areas required by modern life — parking for cars, roads and rooftops, to name a few. Water runs off quickly from these areas, creating big problems downstream, which are magnified if there are only more hard paved areas along the way. It's a domino effect.

Sustainable drainage uses a variety of techniques, such as green roofs and various types of planted areas, to hold water and to slow it down in times of heavy rain or run-off. Plants have the added benefit of cleaning pollution out of storm water along the way. Sustainable drainage systems will increasingly replace traditional sewers, work that will increasingly require the skills of landscape architects.

WATER MANAGEMENT

Landscape architects manage water across all the scales, from large-scale planning of watersheds (whole regions that drain into a river or body of water – the Amazon river basin in Brazil, for example), to water transportation corridors, to localised treatment and management of storm water.

Water management has a number of goals: to keep water safe from pollution, to keep people and property safe from flooding and to protect and restore scenic areas and habitat. Some very important recent work has involved the restoration of wetlands to provide vital habitat for wildlife, insects and plants. Such wetlands can also greatly decrease the danger of floods, as they can absorb water much more effectively than city streets or private gardens.

Water is also an important design element. Like plants, water has qualities that change

over time and in different light and weather conditions. It is capable of producing a wide variety of effects, from a contemplative, placid pond to the exciting spectacle of a great cascade. It appeals to all the senses, to all people of all ages.

PLANTS

Anyone who has ever planted a seed will have watched the moment where the young shoot bursts forth from the soil, stretching itself out and unfurling leaf after leaf. We still know so little about how a seed knows how to become a productive plant that the process might as well be magic. It certainly feels like it.

Plants are a fundamental unit of life on earth, and they support themselves and all animal life through the process of growth, maturation, reproduction, death and decay. It is an endlessly productive cycle.

An understanding of plants has been fundamental to human survival. Hunter-gatherers would have had extensive knowledge of plants, knowing the difference between those that would nourish and those whose consumption spelled death. We can only imagine the first act of planting that led to the creation of agriculture roughly 12,000 years ago. In reality, it was more likely a collective accumulation of plant knowledge over generations that led to organised planting, tending and harvesting.

The birth of agriculture was also the birth of landscape architecture – a shaping of the Earth and its forces to better accommodate the human species. Plants have always been, and always will be, basic to this process.

PLANTS IN NATURE

On both land and in the oceans, plants form a thin layer over the whole surface of the Earth. They are essential to the food chain, using chlorophyll to capture and convert the sun's energy into nutrients. During this process, plants take up carbon dioxide and release oxygen into the atmosphere. This food and fresh air are essential to our existence.

The life cycle of plants is also important to the continuity of all life. When dead and decaying plants decompose, the soil is able to better retain moisture as well as provide nourishment for the next generation of plants. Plants also circulate moisture in the atmosphere, which helps to moderate climate. This is also part of the hydrologic cycle, where water that falls to the ground as rain or snow is returned to the sky to start the whole process again.

For much of human history, we have taken more from these processes than we have returned, and we have reached a stage in both our evolution and the planet's where we must begin collectively to restore the natural equilibrium that has become disrupted nearly to the point of catastrophe.

A natural plant community in the Lake District
Sedums and other alpine plants cling to the naked rock on the fells above Lake Windermere in Britain's Lake District. Here, lichens aid processes of erosion to build soil from stone; when enough has accumulated, small tenacious plants may take hold. Given time, enough soil would form to support a forest.

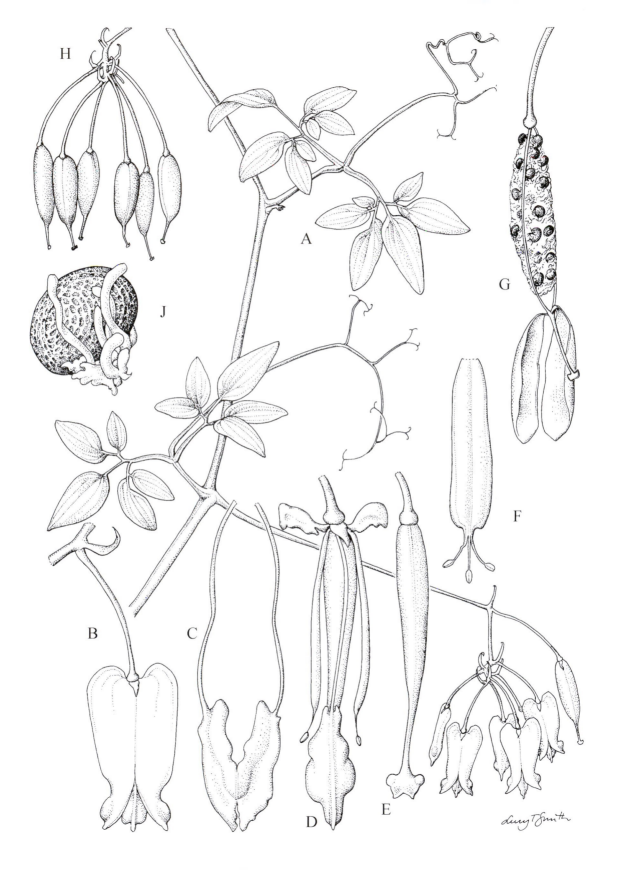

Plant identification and classification

Plants are categorised into groups that have similar characteristics, which gives them a family name, or genus. Within their genus they are distinguished by difference, which assigns them a species. Botanists and horticulturists often use botanical drawings to aid in making these distinctions. *Dactylocapnos ventii* is pictured here in an illustration by renowned botanical illustrator Lucy Smith.

PLANT IDENTIFICATION

As with the earliest hunter-gatherers, it is still a crucial skill to be able to identify one plant from another, for the same basic reason of being able to differentiate between food and poison. For landscape architects, though, it is more important as part of the process of identifying which plants are suitable for a given location or site and, ultimately, for speaking knowledgeably to plant suppliers about their stock.

Plants have both common names and Latin names. The common dandelion, for example, is known by different common names in almost every country in which it is found. It will be universally recognisable, though, by its Latin name, *Taraxacum*. The universal naming of plants only goes back a few centuries, but it has been invaluable to ensure that people the world over have a common language.

PLANTS IN CULTIVATION

Plants give us pleasure, stimulating all the senses. Plants provide us with delicious food, attractive flowers and foliage and delightful scents. This is certainly reason enough for agricultural planting, but why have we come to arrange plants in the landscape in anything other than easy-to-harvest rows?

Plants give us comfort in ways beyond their basic qualities. Trees provide shade, keep strong winds at bay, clean polluted air, moderate temperatures and frame views. Plants can also be used to hold soil in place against the action of erosion, to absorb excess surface water during storms, or to draw contaminants out of polluted soil, among so many other positive attributes.

Plants fall into a few basic categories: trees, shrubs, vines, herbaceous and ground covers. Each of these categories then subdivides endlessly. Trees, for example, divide into evergreen and deciduous, which are then further broken down by leaf type, flower type, fruit type, colour, texture, bark, and where they will or won't grow. This provides an inexhaustible variety of ways to combine plants to make compositions. With the fact that plants change through the seasons and grow larger from year to year, it adds up to the most interesting and dynamic palette of design materials imaginable.

TOPOGRAPHY

The word topography is from the ancient Greek for the 'writing of place'. It refers to the rise and fall of land and the natural and artificial features created by soil, rocks and building. In a more traditional sense, it also refers to the shape of the land created by the type of vegetation on it. For example, grassland would have a different topography from a forest.

In a slightly narrower sense, topography simply means the shape of the land and how it is described on maps using contour lines. Both senses of the word are correct, and both are useful to landscape architecture.

Topography is the result of natural forces acting upon the land, such as when wind forms sand into giant dunes, like those in the Sahara Desert, or when water carves through soil and rock, as can be seen at the Grand Canyon. Gentler examples of topography can often be just as breathtaking, especially when combined with an artfully designed landscape. Even a small hill can provide a commanding view.

In the urban landscape, it is often topography that is most important in defining a city. Imagine San Francisco without its steep streets, Paris without Montmartre (or the Eiffel Tower – itself a topographic feature), Hong Kong without its skyline framed against the Peak, or Tokyo without Mount Fuji.

Landscape architects do not merely work within the context of topography; they also actively shape it.

CONTOURS

Contours are lines used to accurately represent the rise and fall of the land that appear on maps and plans. They represent a line at a constant level elevation (height) traced upon the surface of the land.

As an accurate two-dimensional representation of a three-dimensional surface, contours make it possible to translate information from the map or plan back into a three-dimensional model of a site.

To a skilled map reader, contours can convey much more information than merely the shape of the land. Drainage patterns, which impact on topography through the act of erosion, can be 'read' and can indicate whether a landscape is arid or wet. It is often even possible to make educated guesses about the type of soils or geology in an area simply based upon the patterns of erosion shown by contours.

Landscape architects use contours to create grading plans for a site. These are plans that indicate how the surface of the land is to be shaped (either by heavy machinery or by hand) so that a landscape design may be realised, or so that ground may be cleared and prepared for buildings.

Negev Phosphate Works, Negev Desert, Israel

Spoil from a massive phosphate mine in Israel is used by the landscape architect Shlomo Aronson to create great sculptural earthworks. The terraces literally translate the idea of contours to the site, as the topographic model at bottom right shows.

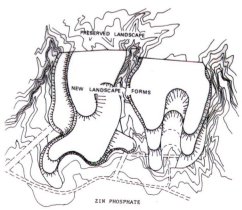

The Fundamentals of Landscape Architecture

Shell Petroleum Headquarters, Rueil-Malmaison, France
Kathryn Gustafson's design for the Shell Headquarters evocatively uses topography both to hide and to frame the building. Waves of turf roll between limestone walls, suggesting both water and the scallop shell of the corporation's logo. Such a landscape is much more complex to design and plan than it would appear, and requires much design exploration using topographic drawings and, in particular, models.

MODELS

A topographic or contour model, whether physical or digital, is an indispensable tool with which to understand a site. The simplest type of topographic model is made of layers of board, such as cardboard or cork, and is made by cutting the boards using contours as a pattern and then gluing each contour level together successively. Built up layer by layer, a topographic model is an accurate scale representation of the slopes to be found on a given site.

It is much easier to understand a site from a model than it is from a map or a plan, and it can easily be understood by someone with no training in reading maps and contours. For the designer, it is a valuable tool to explore drainage patterns, views into and out of a site, wind, weather and microclimates, among many other considerations.

SITE SURVEYS

Built projects begin with the requirement for a contour plan of the site. In order to create a contour plan, it is necessary to obtain an accurate topographic survey of the site's surface and its boundaries.

Surveying uses a variety of different tools and techniques. The theodolite on its tripod is perhaps the most familiar of the instruments involved. It is typically accompanied by a person in a safety vest taking measurements of slopes and angles through the process of triangulation.

Computers, lasers and even robots have made modern surveys much faster and often more accurate. Global Positioning Systems (GPS), which use satellites to fix positions on the Earth's surface, is just one example of the new technology employed in site surveying.

The site survey takes measurements of heights at specific locations (called 'spot elevations') and of slopes, fixing them into context. Once a sufficient number of spot elevations is taken, it is then possible to create a contour plan of the area.

The Fundamentals of Landscape Architecture

LANDSCAPE CHARACTER

Newsstands the world over are packed full of glossy magazines that obsess about human personality, personal appearance and behaviour. If the same bulk of material was produced about the landscape, then we would all have a much better understanding of the world around us. Landscape character is the set of attributes, both tangible and intangible, that define an area, in exactly the same way as looks, personality and behaviour define a person.

Like all people, all landscapes are defined by the sum of their attributes, for better or for worse. Geology, soils, topography and water features such as rivers and lakes are all elements of landscape character. To these elements we can add plants, which can be the most defining elements of a landscape. A forest is a very different place from a prairie. The way animals have used the landscape may change the land's character. Beaver dams, for example, can change a landscape overnight. Animals grazing can also have very visible impacts. However, the human animal often has the most profound influence, with built forms making a strong impact on the landscape, and intensive land uses such as mining or forestry can utterly erase or radically restructure a landscape.

Finally, one of the most important elements of landscape character is the most difficult to define. How we feel about a given place is fundamental to our understanding of it. Is it cosy or vast? Is it beautiful or peaceful? Or is it bizarre or unsettling? Does it feel like home?

WILDERNESS AND NATURE

There are very few true wildernesses left. Just about every inch of the planet is managed in some way or another by humans. This has been the case, though, for longer than one might imagine. Native Americans, for example, burned and cleared the North American prairies for thousands of years. The buffalo haven't roamed in true wilderness for millennia. They have, in fact, benefited from the maintenance and extension of their habitat.

This is not to say that all of nature has been tamed to the whims of people, or that the essence of what it is to be wild has been compromised in any way. Landscape architects work directly at the interface between people and the environment, seeking to strike a balance between the two.

Natural parks and nature reserves are consistent sources of work for landscape architects, from the scale of the local pond to great expanses of tundra. Good management and planning for these areas is vital to preserve the health of the planet and its biodiversity. It is also vital to the human psyche.

We benefit enormously from both direct interaction with the natural world, and the knowledge that wildness and natural majesty are within reach if we desire them.

Every natural landscape has a unique character, from the Serengeti to Patagonia to the Everglades, but it is still immensely useful to draw parallels between places to understand their immense complexity in context.

Yosemite wilderness
The sublime wilderness of California's
Yosemite Valley was preserved as a
natural treasure largely through the
actions of the eminent naturalist
John Muir around the turn of the
last century. Since that time,
landscapes such as this have become
increasingly emblematic of national
and cultural identity.

THE BUILT ENVIRONMENT

The term 'built environment' can be useful to
differentiate inhabited landscapes from 'wild'
landscapes. The built environment includes
everything from agricultural landscapes to
transportation infrastructure. Most often,
though, the term is used in reference to human
urban settlements – cities, towns and villages –
in particular the relationship between built form
and open space in the exterior environment.

In the case of urban environments, landscape
character is the fusion of multiple influences.
Social, cultural, economic, and historic elements
are expressed with a spatial language that draws
upon local topography, vegetation, materials
and climate. Landscape architects are skilled
at reading all these variables in the urban
landscape and making design decisions that are
in harmony with the way people have lived in a
place for generations. Understanding landscape
character is at the heart of making places and at
the heart of landscape architecture.

Housing as a built environment

One type of built environment, that of housing, can take a wide variety of forms depending upon variables such as climate, culture and tradition. The following images show a traditional British village in Dorset, UK; a street in the Marolles district of Brussels, Belgium; a mix of offices and residential areas in Bilbao, Spain; and a roofscape in Tokyo, Japan (facing page).

3

INHABITING THE LANDSCAPE

When we live in a place, make a home in it, a permanent investment, we are said to inhabit it. A good place is one in which we feel comfortable, that fits us like a pair of worn jeans. Landscape architects don't merely make photogenic or sculptural spaces. They make landscapes that are designed for living in, and often the resulting designs are hardly noticeable. Like that pair of jeans, they might not even be noticed unless they're mentioned.

Construction of Ken Smith's Museum of Modern Art Roof Garden, New York
The transformation from a featureless expanse to a place that captures the imagination.

SITE PLANNING AND DEVELOPMENT

'The world is moving into a phase when landscape design may well be recognised as the most comprehensive of the arts.'
Geoffrey Jellicoe

Architects generally have to respond to clients who ask for buildings that stand out and make a statement. However, landscape architects are often at their most successful when their work is least visible. This low-key but incredibly vital approach is apparent in almost every stage of the design process. Architects often begin with grand explorations of form, but landscape architects must intently observe the site, understanding its capabilities, and holding them up against all its possible uses. In landscape architecture it is almost always true that form follows function. This simple formula sounds so easy to resolve, but the landscape presents almost limitless functional possibilities, and the complexity of the intersection of uses is landscape architecture's great challenge.

PROGRAMME DEVELOPMENT

Once an understanding of the site and all its many characteristics and functions has been achieved, the next step is to develop the *programme*. Programme is generally understood as a series of steps that must be carried out, but in the case of a landscape architectural project, it might more usefully be described as a dynamic interrelationship of elements that sets the parameters for design. Understanding the site is the basis for this. The client, who may be

an individual, a community or an organisation, sets forth their needs and requirements. The landscape architect then assesses whether these needs may be accommodated by the site. They also consider whether there are other uses to which the site might be put that might be beneficial. With this balance in place, the landscape architect may then communicate clear goals and objectives for the site design.

With objectives in place, the designer may then begin to test the relationships between uses and the site. Schematic drawings are a useful tool for this, and this is usually known as the schematic design phase. The schematic phase is where the bulk of conceptual development occurs. At this point in the programme development, it is usually useful to study projects by other designers to see how they have responded to similar issues. This is known as 'comparative analysis' or 'precedent study'. Programme development generally leads to the production of a conceptual plan that may then be presented to the client for approval.

To put it as simply as possible, programme development is the act of fitting possible activities and requirements to a site, and deciding how these uses work together in the available space.

SITE SELECTION

On almost any project, landscape architects need to be involved from the very beginning. Landscape architects provide the big picture – and there is little use in waiting for it until the end of a project. For every site, there are ideal uses, and for every use there is an ideal site. If a client has a project to propose, a landscape architect has all the skills to help find the perfect spot. Say, for example, that the client is a university

1. PROGRAM   2. HABITAT   3. CIRCULATION

   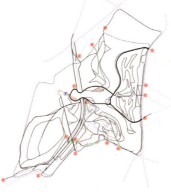

that has outgrown its old facilities and needs to move to a new campus. Naturally, this is a use that would require a considerable amount of space. A wide variety of building types and uses would need to be accommodated, from science laboratories to libraries, commons buildings and dormitories. The site would need to have excellent public transport, as students cannot be expected to own cars. A university would also need to demonstrate that its building is as enlightened as its thinking, making sustainability a primary concern.

To accomplish these goals, a landscape architect uses a combination of tools. An ideal schematic might be created. This is a drawing that shows all the possible activities and uses that the client has set forth, and how they might be arranged to complement each other perfectly. The commons bar, for example, ought to be close to the dormitories, but not so close as to cause disruption to those who do not wish to partake in any festivities. Remote sensing is an important part of the site-selection process, and this includes the use of maps, aerial photographs, satellite imagery, and Geographic Information Systems (GIS). Finally, there is no substitute for a physical visit to the actual site.

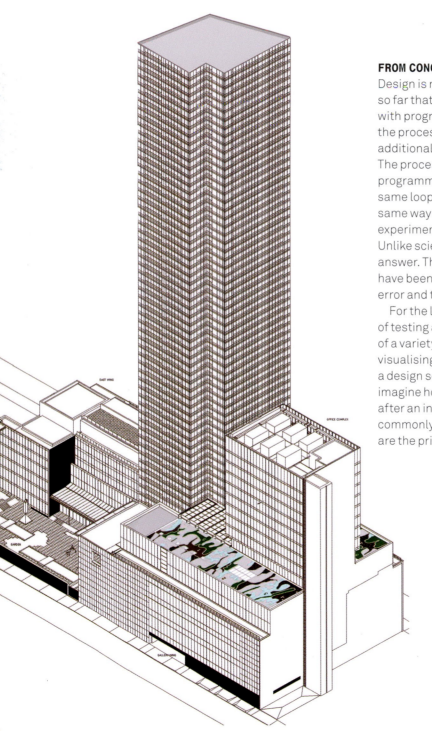

FROM CONCEPT TO DESIGN

Design is not a linear process. We have seen so far that site inventory and analysis overlap with programme development, for example, and the process of development always points up additional research that must be undertaken. The process circles back on itself. From programme development to construction, the same loops occur. Design involves testing, in the same way that a scientist might make repeated experiments to achieve an answer to a question. Unlike science, however, there is no one correct answer. There are only workable solutions that have been arrived at by a combination of trial and error and the designer's own unique voice.

For the landscape architect, the process of testing and retesting means making use of a variety of materials and techniques for visualising the site and its issues. In order to test a design solution, the designer must be able to imagine how the site would look and function after an intervention – 'design move' is the term commonly used for this. Drawing and modelling are the primary tools employed.

Museum of Modern Art Roof Garden, New York, Ken Smith

Ken Smith's design for the MoMA Roof Garden was based upon the camouflage pattern found in a pair of shorts. Camouflage is an imitation of nature and the highly artificial environment of the museum rooftop in the heart of Manhattan is an apt location for an imitation of an imitation. Many variations were tried before the final design was selected.

THE DESIGN PROCESS

Despite the fact that the design process is reiterative and cyclical, it is still possible to define stages. One must imagine that the designer will move between each of these stages as needed. This sequence from concept to design applies to all the architectures as well as to engineering.

Commission – When a job is commissioned, the client issues the brief for the project, defining the goals, expected activities and requirements and the services to be provided.

Research – The site inventory process compiles data for the site, including maps, images, historical records and other documents. Precedent studies are also included.

Analysis – The qualities of the site and the requirements of the brief are examined to determine opportunities. Analysis includes programme development, which leads on to synthesis.

Synthesis – The schematic stage culminates in the design stage, requiring a great deal of communication with the client or sometimes community consultation. The inspirational stage in which the design gels is contained within synthesis.

Construction – The final design is detailed in construction documents so that it may be built. The landscape architect usually supervises the construction process.

Operation – Monitoring a design's success is important for any practice – much is to be learned at this stage. Visits are made to the site after completion; any faults are rectified and necessary adjustments are made. Sometimes, landscape architects remain on contract for maintenance for many years after a design's completion.

THE VIEW OF THE LANDSCAPE

'Landscape and image
are inseparable.'
James Corner

To many, the view of the landscape and the
landscape itself are synonymous. A 'landscape'
might be either the landscape itself or a picture
of it. However, landscape architects know it to be
so much more, appealing to all the senses and
composed of a great variety of elements, both
seen and unseen. Sight, though, is the primary
sense we use to encounter our environment and
to make judgements about it; the view of the
landscape, therefore, is of primary importance
to the designer.

The view of the landscape is more than just
a pretty picture. Views in the landscape are
dynamic, in motion, and they help us to orient
ourselves as well as to inform us of the type of
space we are in and how it is to be used.

VIEW

The landscape architect must consider views
from three different angles: views from the
site, views within the site; and views of the site.
Each of these is important to how an individual
comprehends the site and all must be taken into
account for the design to be successful.

Views themselves may have many functions.
Views may be framed, by trees or by a window.
They may serve as a backdrop, a setting against
which action takes place. Views may serve as
a setting for architecture, or in turn may be
enhanced by architecture. Buildings in an urban
setting play a particularly important part in
framing or directing views.

Views may form the basis of a site for
meditation or relaxation, but they may also be
used to draw people into motion, to provide them
with a visual goal that impels them to explore.
While exploring, they might also discover that
views have a way of unfolding, of being concealed
and revealed when the viewer is in motion.

VISTA

A vista is a view that is framed or confined.
A picture window, for example, is used to best
effect when it very carefully centres a view,
editing out extraneous detail such as poles
and power lines.

City vistas are captured in the same way.
One of London's most exciting vistas is through
an archway at Piccadilly Circus, in which a long
view captures the Victoria Tower of the Houses
of Parliament and the Duke of York's Column at
Waterloo Place. Under the arch, an entrance to
the Underground displays the ubiquitous bar
and circle logo, and red double-decker buses
lumber by behind. It is a vista that captures the
essence of London in a glimpse, and it is far
from accidental. It is a work of urban landscape
design, enhanced by architecture and animated
by the hustle and bustle of a great city.

Hans Dieter Schaal, The Garden at the Villa Liebfried

Placed in the overgrown vegetation of the grounds of the Villa Liebfried, which was destroyed in the Second World War, Schaal's deeply considered design barely touches the ground at all. It introduces lightweight wooden structures into the garden to provide destinations and to frame views. In one case, an apparent overlook turns out to be an illusion, framing a view only in the visitor's imagination.

AXIS AND SYMMETRY

An axis might be referred to as the 'spine' of a site, and it is usually a broad path or roadway, often flanked by buildings. It may be straight, curved or sinuous, but it never branches, always holding a hard line. It is a powerful, primary, unifying feature in the landscape to which all else is subservient, though it may be crossed or paralleled by other axes. Baroque gardens, such as Versailles, use this feature as the organising feature in a landscape in which all elements are symmetrical – mirror images reflected across the spine. The symbolism involved in these powerful, symmetrical gardens is about the dominion of humans over nature.

Symmetry can be inflexible, though, and its rigid formality has a dehumanising quality to it. There is no need for an axis to be accompanied by symmetry. The Broad Walk, the primary axis at The Regent's Park in London, hugs the side of the park, which is a flattened, ovoid shape, and it is crossed by a strong secondary axis, but is also joined by numerous meandering paths and diagonals. It provides a long promenade that organises the park, but doesn't prevent people from rambling at will and feeling free to relax.

THE CINEMATIC LANDSCAPE

The first half of the twentieth century, especially the 1930s and 1940s, might be seen as the golden age of road building. The motor car had added new glamour to the romance of the open road, and cinema was the perfect new medium with which to express this love affair. Landscape architects, especially in the United States, were employed to design and sculpt roads that would provide pleasurable and scenic drives. Film became a metaphor for how the views might unfold and be modulated over the course of a road, and the car window mimicked the frame of the camera as it captured the moving vista. What a shame that speed and flow, rather than pleasure and romance are all too often the only criteria for road building today.

Any other mode of ground transportation, however, from walking to rail travel, can also provide the same effect. Views can, by turns, be concealed and revealed, unfolding or unrolling, creating anticipation, surprise, and a setting for a thrilling arrival. The landscape is dynamic, cinematic, and panoramic. And all in vivid colour.

The Blue Ridge Parkway, Eastern USA
Proof that the romance with the car was not at odds with a romance with the landscape, Stanley W Abbott's designs for Blue Ridge Parkway created a cinematic sequence of exquisite unfolding views for the motorist. Sometimes, it is the road itself that is the focus of the view, as this remarkable viaduct shows.

LANDSCAPE PLANTING

Plants are the landscape architect's stock in trade. While it is no longer necessary for each individual landscape architect to exhibit a mastery of horticulture, plants still form the most visible and structural elements of the environment, and every firm must be able to provide expertise in working with plants. Unlike buildings, which begin to age and decay from the moment they are finished, plants in the landscape grow, improve and mature. Within the shorter timescale of the seasons, they provide a display that is ever changing and exciting, from the first flush of spring to the bare branches of winter.

Landscape architecture often suffers from the misconception that it is a profession employed to 'shrub it up', as though the landscape is the parsley garnish to architecture's perfectly formed omelette. Worse, landscape architects are sometimes asked to cover up faults or screen out horrors that could have been better designed from the beginning. It is vital that landscape architects are employed on projects early to avoid such disasters. This unfortunate situation has caused many landscape architects to try to disassociate themselves from planting design, rather than to take pride in the enormous range for design that plants offer.

Plants are important not just for their visual amenity, but for the other services and benefits they provide. Vegetation may be used for erosion control, to manage surface water and for climate control, to name a few examples.

COMPOSITION

A common term for the range of plants used in a design is the 'plant palette'. This is an appropriate term. In the same way that a painter might choose colours and textures of paint to apply to a canvas, the landscape architect has a rich selection of plants to choose from that will be appropriate to any site. Designers with practice in planting will often develop a selection of plants that they know well and which they can rely on to perform time and time again. This can be as much a signature for the designer as a practical way of working from day to day.

Landscape architects create planting plans for sites, using the same principles of design applied to the 'hard' elements of the site, such as walls and paving. The designer will test planting designs on the planting plan by sketching them, either as a perspective drawing or by drawing a more technical section through the plan. Trees, being the largest and most structural of plants, generally form the backbone of any planting plan, with shrubs providing structure at a more human scale. Other plant types include ground covers, vines, and herbaceous plants.

Plant compositions can follow many different styles. Capability Brown's style was to plant groupings of trees in a park-like setting of rolling lawns. Plantings may be done in sweeps, with random spacing, or with rigid geometric spacing in a grid or as an allée. It is also possible to specify maintenance methods that may have a profound effect on the form of plants, such as shearing shrubs into hedges or topiary, or pleaching or pollarding trees.

Gardens of the Great Basin, Chicago Botanic Garden, Glencoe, Illinois
The firm of Oehme and van Sweden are notable for their robust, painterly approach to landscape planting. The Gardens of the Great Basin is a garden based around a circuit of experiences, including paths, bridges and vistas. The plant choices are typical to American Midwestern gardens.

Planting Plan, Cogels Park
The planting plan is a construction document that provides detailed information for the contractor on specific plants, their location, quantity, size and method of planting.

PLANT CHARACTERISTICS FOR DESIGN

Form – the shape and 'habit' of a plant, such as weeping trees

Size – the mature height and width of a plant

Texture – leaves and branches can be fine, medium or coarse

Colour – the colour of leaves, bark and flowers must all be taken into account

PLANT SUITABILITY FOR SITE

Soil – specific plants will generally have a preference for a particular type of soil

Moisture – some plants will tolerate drought, while others have a limitless thirst

Climate – wind and extremes of temperature will dictate the extent of a plant palette

Microclimate – specific site characteristics, such as sun and shade, will also affect plant choice

THE SEASONS

In many areas of the globe, there is little change from season to season. Equatorial regions and polar regions offer variations on a single theme – hot, hotter and hottest, or cold, colder and frigid. This is not to say that a wide range of plants does not exist for either area, but there is less dramatic change, if any at all, from month to month.

The most noticeable change that the seasons bring in temperate climates is visual. The vivid, sometimes electric greens brought by new growth in the spring rains; the parched browns and yellows of summer; the fiery shades of autumn; and the stark contrasts of winter. The coincidence in the change of climatic conditions and plant conditions can often be fortuitous in other ways. In winter, when every drop of sunlight is precious, the trees are bare to let as much of the light filter through as possible, while in the summer, the trees are lush with leaves to provide shade from the heat of the sun.

Planting design has time on its side, with the long-term change and maturation of planted landscapes providing pleasure and variety over many years, and with four seasons a year to ensure that there is constant interest. All the variables involved in plant design may sound overwhelming, but the rewards of learning manifest themselves in time as well.

The Fundamentals of Landscape Architecture

FLOW: CIRCULATION AND ACCESS

'A lot of my works deal with a passage, which is about time. I don't see anything that I do as a static object in space. It has to exist as a journey in time.'
Maya Lin

It is not merely the seasons that animate landscapes. Picture books glorifying gardens or architecture will often show them as completely static, frozen in time, and will curiously exclude people from the image. There are more than a few images in this book that are guilty of the same omission. Landscapes are animated by wind, by light, by birds and bees and the weather. One of the most fascinating elements that animates the landscape is us. People are always in motion, using a great variety of methods of transport. Landscapes are built to accommodate people in motion, and even when people are at rest, they tend to watch everyone else move around. People-watching may be the most universal pastime of all.

Balancing the needs (and speeds) of people in motion is a big job. Landscape architects work with town planners, engineers and transportation planners, amongst other professions, to accomplish all the fine-tuning that is required to make circulation work. The flow of circulation is often likened to the flow of water, and, indeed, it can often seem just such an inexorable force. Thundering traffic on a busy arterial can be every bit as intimidating as white-water rapids in full flow. Traffic flows often converge and quicken in the same way that water does. The little tributaries of side streets trickle out into the fatter flows of the main roads.

Containing these flows, channelling them, allowing them to pool and eddy, is a major task of the landscape architect.

FLOW AND MOTION

Moving through a designed space is more than just experiencing it. It is putting it to work in the same way that a machine can be put to work. Space is inert until it is put into motion by occupation, or occupied with motion. Space is also shaped by the circulation on a site, either by what the designer anticipates will occur, or the existing patterns of circulation that the designer must accommodate. New York's Central Park, for example, is set into the existing grid of streets, requiring the park to be crossed by a major street at regularly spaced intervals. These streets are sunken below the park level, with paths crossing on bridges above. The paths themselves are separated into a hierarchy, with broad, gently snaking paths taking faster, more direct pedestrian and bicycle traffic, while a filigree of smaller paths meander through glades and over hills for strollers in search of a more leisurely experience. Many sites will have similar levels of complexity even if they are at a much smaller scale.

Space Syntax, the London pedestrian route map concept

Space Syntax has gained a reputation working with movement and flow in the city. Their concept for a pedestrian route map is based on the logic of Harry Beck's London Underground map, which was patterned upon an electrical circuit diagram. It allows individual pedestrians to possess a complete, rather than fragmentary, idea of a chosen route.

The Fundamentals of Landscape Architecture

Legend:

Waterfront routes	Shopping route
Monuments routes	Northern route
Euston/Marylebone City Roads Boulevard	Central route
Park routes	Broad Walk
Farringdon/Islington route	Serpentine Route
Monuments route	Nash Ramblas

- Underground station
- Mainline rail station
- Distance to next junction
- Visitor attraction
- Pedestrian decision-making point
- Future route

WORK IN PROGRESS

PEDESTRIANS

Pedestrians have the richest experience of the landscape. Walking speeds allow the individual to take in the maximum amount of detail in the landscape in a trajectory that constantly reveals and modulates. There are different modes of walking that change the nature of the experience as well. Strolling is a different experience from striding, and then there is the jerky and discontinuous motion of the walker who moves between points of interest – the window-shopper or the birdwatcher, for example. Walking for pleasure and walking with a specific destination in mind are also very different.

Most pedestrian experience is on a very mundane day-to-day basis, and may be a simple triangle between work, home and the shops. These familiar routes are populated with small landmarks that might be unnoticed. A favourite spot to perch and rest, for example, or an old advertisement fading into the bricks. The many textures of a place, and of the lived experience of it, should all fall within consideration.

CARS

Cars present, perhaps, the biggest single challenge in landscape architecture. They are lethal, poisonous and bulky, but they provide us with convenience (or at least the illusion of it). They are also important markers of class, status, power and prowess. Cars have torn up the fabric of historic cities and created deserts of paved space in communities designed with cars in mind. An immense amount of effort and expense is put into designing urban environments around the needs of people in cars, and to preserve the safety of those on the street.

There is an endless tug of war between the needs of cars and the needs of people. Traffic engineers are concerned with flows and speed, and of keeping people out of the way. Landscape architects are concerned with making places for people and for preserving the ecological integrity of the environment. Fortunately, our message seems to be coming across, aided in no small part by the dwindling supply of fuel and the ever more visible degradation of the environment.

Some car-related issues appear again and again. Everyone will be familiar with the difficulty of finding parking, the desire for which continues to eat away at public open space. The extent to which pedestrians should be separated from traffic continues to be debated, with one camp erecting barriers and fences, and another tearing them down and relying on everyone's sense of responsibility.

PUBLIC TRANSPORTATION AND OTHER MODES OF TRANSPORT

Our planet's resources are not limitless, and therefore we can be assured that travelling communally on public transportation is likely to be the wave of the future. Freight, as well, has been distributed by trucks, but we will probably need to return to a reliance on bulk transport by rail and water in the future. We will also need to rely upon our local resources more.

A good transportation structure is central to communities, and the transport should not only be effective, safe and reliable, but the routes should also be pleasurable and scenic. The view of the city from a train always seems to comprise the most dejected set of back walls and dereliction, yet trains almost always connect city centre to city centre, a luxury that

Hamilton Baillie Associates, Winchester City Centre

Hamilton Baillie are keen proponents of the principles of 'shared space'; street markings are minimised or eliminated to create mutual awareness and responsibility amongst all road users. The approach has been particularly successful in many cases, with significant reductions in road speeds and accidents. The project for Winchester City Centre incorporates some of these principles.

air travel will never manage. Modern trams are clean, sleek and quiet, and, although expensive to install, are much more orderly and effective than buses – the convenience and environmental improvements pay off for generations.

Many other transportation solutions exist. Some have been tried and found wanting, such as the original monorail, but its contemporary equivalent, the high-speed maglev, or magnetically levitating train, shows huge promise. People movers and driverless cars have also been tried successfully. It is also difficult to underestimate the value of the humble bicycle and its endlessly renewable energy source.

STRUCTURES AND HABITATION

A simple boundary – a wall, a fence or an enclosure – is enough for us to understand that a space has been defined for human use or inhabitation. A land divided into fields is clearly inhabited, as is a garden, which might be bounded by a fence or hedge. Public squares are surrounded on all sides by important buildings. Certain types of enclosure are appropriate to certain types of spaces. A grand fountain on a rectangle of marble paving slabs, completed with ornate lamp standards and a grid of trees, would simply fail to be a public square if it was in the middle of a field, surrounded by a strand of barbed wire. This sounds ridiculous, but it does so because we are so conditioned to certain types of spaces that this understanding is often quite intuitive.

The relationship between structures and space has an important effect on the activities that may occur there. The best way for a designer to understand how public spaces work is to observe them first hand; watch how people behave, how they enjoy a space, and how they use the street furniture. Landscape architects design the outdoor spaces where people live, work and play, and where community comes together. It is vital to remember to take the time to relax by walking in the park or nursing a glass of wine in a street cafe. Just tell people you're hard at work, observing.

BUILDING ARCHITECTURE AND LANDSCAPE

Buildings and landscape come together as three-dimensional geometric form. We talk about the spaces created within the landscape in geometric terms. There is also a vital geometric difference between urban design in landscape architecture and town planning. Town planning is concerned with areas, whereas landscape architecture is concerned with volumes. The space of a plaza can be termed a volume, but on a map or plan it appears as an area. Volumes are also modulated as we move through space, with views opening out, or gaps between buildings set closer or further apart.

The volume of a space, defined by its enclosure, can communicate a great deal about its intentions. Tiananmen Square in Beijing, built by Mao Zedong, is the largest public square in the world, covering 40 hectares. It is not a place for community to come together, but rather for the display of power and for military parades. The Grand Place in Brussels is also a showcase of power, with the ornate and gilded buildings of the city's mediaeval guilds arrayed around it. However, the scale of the space is comfortable and convivial, and on summer evenings, people sit in groups on the cool paving slabs and share drinks, talking well into the night.

The volumes of space are defined by planes, and we refer to these as the 'ground plane', the 'overhead plane' and the 'verticals'. This is easiest to picture in an interior space, such as a

Olin, Robert F. Wagner Jr. Park, New York, New York
Laurie Olin's design for this busy New York site steps down carefully in scale from the surrounding tall buildings to provide a welcoming and friendly enclosure. The rectangular lawn, reminiscent of a billiard table, is enclosed by a low bench that makes a perfect place for parents to perch while their children play on the lawn.

hall with columns. The floor is the ground plane, the ceiling the overhead plane, while the walls and columns are verticals. Substitute earth and sky for floor and ceiling, and the concept transfers nicely to the outdoors.

DEFINING SPACE

The physical, geometric spaces we inhabit would be dull indeed if they were simply collections of shapes. Culture, which expresses itself in locality, and which in turn is expressed by place, brands our spaces and our built forms with identity and character. In the city, this is often built up over great spans of time, and a new building requires careful integration into a fabric that has been woven slowly. Building architects are currently obsessed with creating unique buildings that stand out, but if the architects of the past had not realised that their buildings were part of an overall urban texture, then we would have visual chaos in our cities, with every building shouting to be heard. It is important to see buildings as part of a landscape context, rather than as ends unto themselves.

Beauty is intuitive. There are no rules for proportion or measure; there are only conventions that are dictated by the physical limits of building materials and the scale of the human body. Visual rhythm, spacing, and the relationship between building masses and open space are all decided upon in design. They may be integrated within existing context, psychologically comfortable or be able to accommodate and fit the human body.

Olin, Bryant Park, New York, New York
The classic formalism of Bryant Park would be threateningly overshadowed by some of the newer tall buildings that are adjacent, were it not for the grid of trees that provides a strong overhead plane for the site, and the clear relationship of the central lawn to the imposing, but not overwhelming, scale of the New York Public Library, at the centre of the image.

COMMUNITY PLANNING

'Everyone has the right to walk from one end of the city to the other in secure and beautiful spaces. Everybody has the right to go by public transport. Everybody has the right to an unhampered view down their street, not full of railings, signs and rubbish.'
Richard Rogers

Individual people can be prickly or difficult to fathom, they could be generous and welcoming. What is true of individuals is true many times over for communities, which are, after all, groups of individuals. Government officials love to talk about 'making communities inclusive', but communities are really actually exclusive. They need to be defined by what and who they exclude in order to have a common language amongst the individuals. What those officials really mean is that communities should not have life so difficult that they are forced on to the defensive, where they might be hostile to those who are different.

First and foremost to creating strong communities is eliminating poverty and inequality. Landscape architects come into the picture by helping to erase the markers of poverty and inequality in the built environment. People are not made evil and hateful by their environments, but it does not help when everything that can be seen is a reminder of the daily adversity they face. Good community design and planning can be a powerful statement of optimism and hope, and with the support of good social planning and economic improvement, it can provide a better quality of life for all.

Some communities are already beautiful and function well. Planning for these communities can be just as much a challenge, as any change might be seen to compromise the well-being that has been achieved. Every place, though, needs change over time, as patterns and modes of living change. All communities deserve good design. All communities, in fact, should have a right to good design.

BoO1 City of Tomorrow, Malmø, Sweden
BoO1 was developed as part of an international housing exhibition in 2001, and brought together enlightened professionals to design sustainable forms and patterns for the future. The result is a gracious development at a very human scale. Great neighbourhoods are not often built from scratch, however, and the question of housing for the future will certainly involve retrofitting existing neighbourhoods.

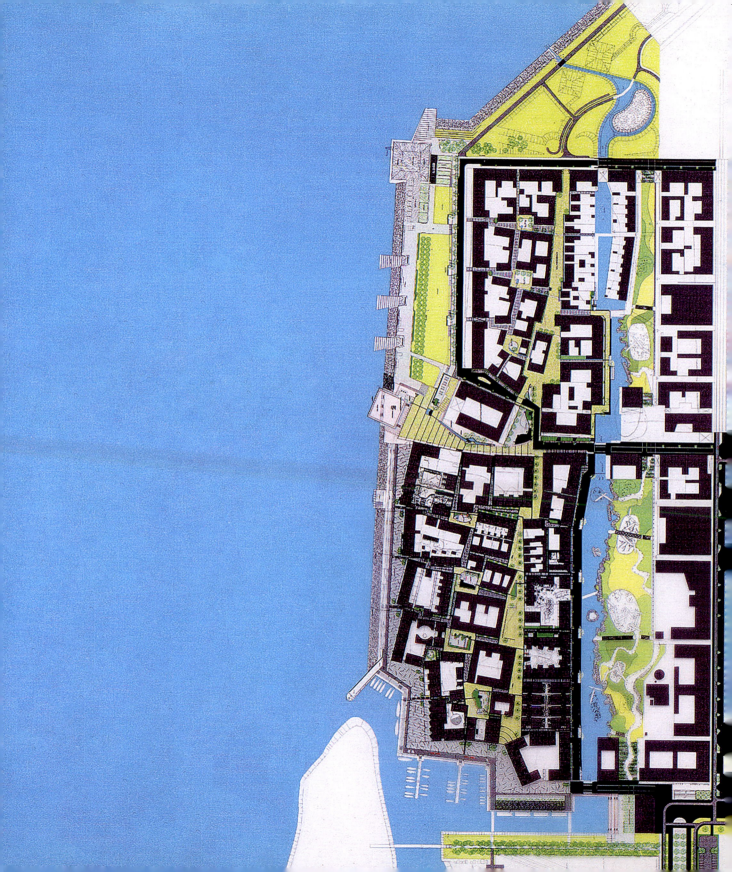

Bo01 City of Tomorrow, Malmø, Sweden

In northern climates, a spot of sun will bring everyone outdoors. The waterfront boardwalk at Malmø provides an opportunity for people to stroll, to relax, or to meet.

DESIGNING FOR COMMUNITIES

Technology is now uniting us with easy communication available via mobile phones and social networking websites. At the same time, it is separating us from each other, as we are often so busy communicating with each other electronically and listening to our iPods that we might as well live in bubbles. Communities still exist in physical space as well as virtual space, and there are certain physical characteristics that are necessary for any neighbourhood, which must be considered in the design.

As communities interact in public, physical access is hugely important. Communities should be walkable. Amenities and necessities such as shops, parks, cafés, pubs, swimming pools and community gardens should all be within a short walk from home. A good network of footpaths through houses, with a view of the street, ensures that there are plenty of people around and plenty of eyes on the street to keep everyone safe. Public outdoor spaces, such as parks, gardens, sporting grounds, squares and promenades, should be available for all, but in proportion. Too many facilities can be impossible to maintain, and an abundance of neglected parks is anything but an asset.

Good community design can do a great deal to enhance quality of life and to fight isolation and crime.

SUSTAINABLE COMMUNITY

'Sustainability' is a slippery term. It has been abused by politicians and advertisers, seeking to align themselves with a feel-good green message, but often without delivering the goods. It is not a new concept, though. It used to be called good, thoughtful, problem-solving design that is built to last, which gives more than it takes at every stage. Good design and sustainable design are one and the same thing. When we talk about sustainable communities, then the same common sense rationale can be applied. A sustainable community is one where people feel safe, welcome, and know their neighbours. It is built well, easy to get to, and has good shops, jobs, and educational and recreational opportunities.

Creating sustainable communities is about creating a better society with equal distribution of wealth, health and hope. Combined Heat and Power (CHP) is a good example of one of the physical ways that design can contribute directly to more sustainable communities. CHP operates on the principle that the generation of electricity also generates heat, both of which can be used locally by communities. Big power stations only benefit big companies, as much electricity is lost in transmission. CHP allows communities direct control over some of their most basic necessities, while lowering costs for all. A small power station will heat homes and power them on a local grid. It is an elegant example of how working together and sharing, a concept at the heart of a community, can be assisted by enlightened engineers and designers. And it seems so very much like common sense, but it takes vision, planning and a lot of hard work.

4

REPRESENTATION

A representation is an image that stands for or symbolises an idea, concept or elements of the physical world. When we speak of representation in architecture, we speak of the process of showing and looking at a site, showing and testing design ideas and communicating an idea to an audience and a builder. There are many different materials and techniques for representation, and each one of them offers a different way of imagining a site and the design options for it. Drawing materials can allow the designer to 'feel' elements of the site, as they can stand in for textures, emotions, or moods.

Despite the fact that computers can now be employed in all stages of design, there is still no substitute for a broad command of all types of materials and methods for representation and the space in which to experiment and explore. The broader the range of tools, the more expansive the imagination, the designer's stock-in-trade.

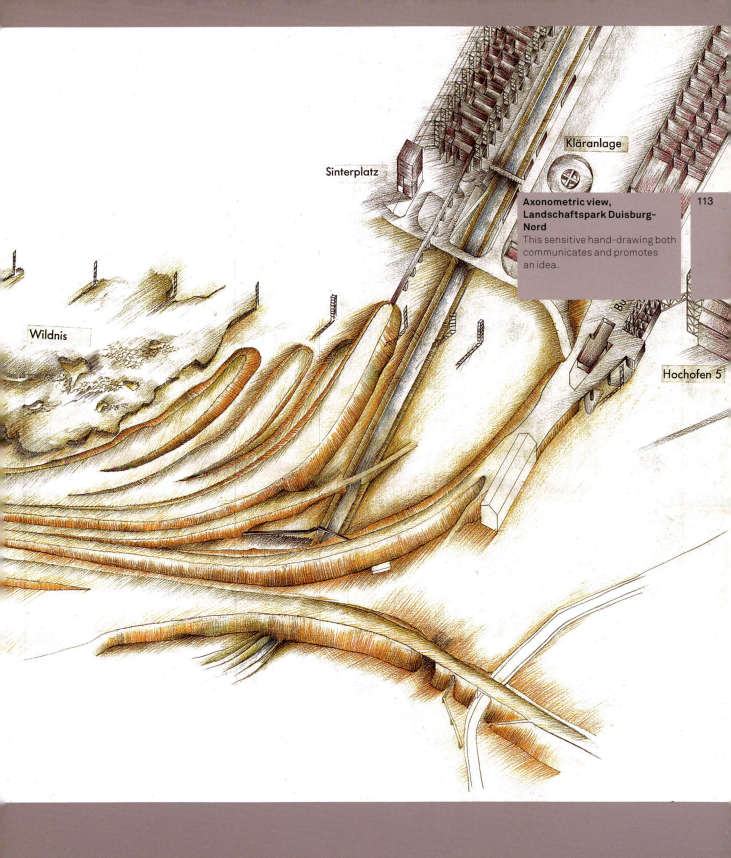

Sinterplatz

Kläranlage

Wildnis

Hochofen 5

Axonometric view, Landschaftspark Duisburg-Nord
This sensitive hand-drawing both communicates and promotes an idea.

THE SKETCH

114

4. REPRESENTATION

THE SKETCH | ›ORTHOGRAPHIC PROJECTION

'I prefer drawing to talking. Drawing is faster, and leaves less room for lies.'
Le Corbusier

A sketch is a drawing that can be executed quickly, to capture the essence of a place or an idea. It is a quick way to work through and test ideas, or to communicate on the fly. A great number of breakthrough drawings have been made in designers' sketchbooks, or even on cocktail napkins over drinks. Sketches often capture the moment of inspiration.

Sketches provide a sort of visual shorthand, often reducing a key element down to a single line or figure. Cartoons are a type of sketch that do just this, and often with an incredible economy of gesture. An upwardly curving line and two dots surrounded by a circle is a smiling face, but more, it symbolises a positive attitude, a benign state of mind, and has even been the marker for a subculture. A great deal of information and meaning can be packed into the simplest of images.

OBSERVATIONAL SKETCHES

An observational sketch is a drawing of a view that the artist or designer wishes to represent. The simplest way to capture a view is probably to point a camera at it and snap the shutter. The camera, though, does not edit an image to show what is important to the human eye. It is limited in the way it frames an image and in the type of lens that is in use. Pointing a camera is a way of looking, but not necessarily of *seeing*.

Observational sketches are a healthy activity in many ways. They get people outdoors. They offer an excuse to simply sit and watch. Most importantly, they are healthy for design because they give the designer a tool to observe the site over time, and to understand how it is used and appreciated. They are a method of recording the site and for making judgements about it. The sketch is then a log of the moment and the observations that aid the designer's memory, which helps to communicate ideas to others.

CONCEPTUAL SKETCHES

A conceptual sketch is an economic means of communicating or exploring an idea. A conceptual sketch usually takes the form of a diagram or a schematic. A bubble diagram is a standard example, and these are used frequently in landscape architecture, often to show the relationships between various uses on different parts of a site.

Conceptual sketches are also a useful method for showing the connections between spaces, uses and flows. A conceptual sketch generally will avoid too much specificity in what it shows, as a flexible understanding of relationships is more helpful to design in the early stages. Conceptual sketches will often end up forming the backbone of a finished design, and are often extremely useful in conveying the meaning of a design to a client or the public.

Concept sketch, streetscape design, London
A simple sketch with bold imagery allows the designer to clearly articulate a design idea to both themselves and to a client. Using a consistent and coherent concept through the design helps a client gain a better grasp of what might be a very complex set of spatial and temporal considerations.

ANALYTICAL SKETCHES

Analytical sketches are often made on site during the initial phase of site inventory and analysis. Like conceptual sketches, they are useful for showing the relationship between spaces, uses and flows, but they may be developed to a much greater degree of specificity. Natural characteristics of the site may be taken into account, such as the direction of prevailing winds, the presence of important natural assets, such as particularly attractive trees, or, perhaps, an area inhabited by an endangered species. Physical and human characteristics of the site can be mapped against the natural in order to provide a comprehensive picture of the site's relationships and its character.

Analytical sketches are helpful at any stage in the design process, as they are a primary tool in exploring the dynamic interplay of elements that may be found on any site.

THE SKETCHBOOK

The sketchbook is more than a tool for design. It might more properly be viewed as an extension of the designer's body, brain and imagination. The designer, through training, becomes conversant in using words and images simultaneously and flexibly in the design process, and the sketchbook is often where this work takes place. The sketchbook is generally small, light and portable, travelling everywhere and offering clean, blank pages hungry to be filled.

The sketchbook is particularly useful for documenting the process of design and showing the trajectory of the designer's ideas. It is a personal space that can be filled with messy, questing drawings, half-answered questions and sudden revelations. It accepts a great variety of techniques for drawing, and just about anything that can be done to a sheet of paper can happen in a sketchbook.

Pages from a sketchbook

All types of sketches, notes and text find their way into a designer's sketchbook. Here drawings and collage show parts of the landscape architect Ed Wall's exploration of a site.

Site analysis drawing, Old Lodge Farm, Chelmsford, England

While a site analysis sketch is often scribbled on a plan on site, these sketches can also be prepared as more deliberate presentation drawings. Mapping the various influences on a site on to a single plan is an important part of the process of understanding its dynamics.

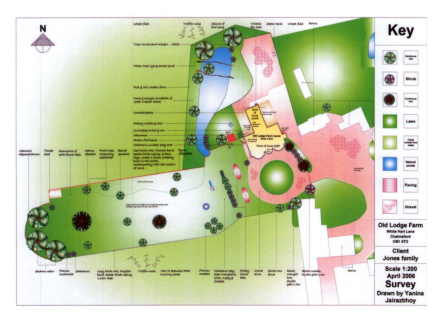

ORTHOGRAPHIC PROJECTION

Orthographic projection is measured drawing producing a 'true' representation of a site or object that is to scale. It is also called technical drawing. Orthographic projection generally means creating a two-dimensional representation of a three-dimensional site or object. Builders, following instructions from a designer, will consult these accurate drawings so that they know exactly where and how to build each element of a project. The man in the hard hat with the plans in his hands? He's holding an orthographic projection.

A *plan* is a two-dimensional measured horizontal drawing. It places the viewer in an imaginary position above the site or object looking straight down at it without any distortion. A *section* is a vertical slice through the site or object, just like a slice of bread. It shows the exact height and width of every object it encounters. It appears on the plan as a simple line where the two planes intersect. Plans and sections are the two primary types of orthographic projections.

SCALE

Scale is the medium through which it is possible to create orthographic projections. It is generally expressed as a fraction or a ratio. It is used to produce a drawing at a specific fraction of the full-size dimensions of an object. A scale drawing at life size would be at a scale of 1:1 or 1 / 1, whereas a drawing at half life size would be at a ratio of 1:2 or 1 / 2.

SCALE

The following scales are merely indicative, and are intended only to give a feeling for the range of scales and the size of site to which they would be applied. These scales would produce drawings of presentation or map size.

1:1	Actual size
1:10	Bus shelter
1:100	Garden
1:500	City park
1:1,000	Neighbourhood
1:20,000	City
1:200,000	County
1:1,000,000	Country
1:5,000,000	Europe
1:50,000,000	World

In order to fit a large site on to a standard-sized piece of paper, landscape architects often use much more 'zoomed-out' scales such as 1:200 or 1:1,000. A site at the scale of 1:1,000 would be 1,000 times smaller than life size, and this scale might be used for a project covering a significant area, such as a large housing development. Maps zoom out even further. The city of Florence can be well covered at the scale of 1:12,500, but all of Italy might need a scale of 1:1,000,000.

PLANS

A plan represents the site as it is measured on the surface of the ground, registering the horizontal distances between objects. It is a two-dimensional measured technical drawing. Plans are excellent tools for communicating a design, but are usually very poor tools for the work of design itself. Because they place the viewer in

Section drawings

These simple sections show terraces being built. The dump truck in the image helps establish scale.

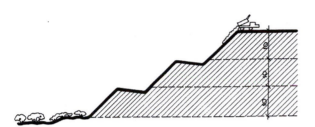

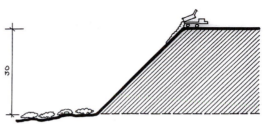

an unnatural position, looking straight down on the site from an imaginary height, they lead to a tendency to simply make patterns on the ground, rather than creating three-dimensional spaces for people. Because of this top-down view, they create an illusion of power that reduces the humans in a design scheme to mere pawns in a board game. However, plans are essential to ensure that design proposals explored in other types of drawings are correctly proportioned, fitting on the site in the manner intended.

SECTIONS

A section shows the heights and widths of objects encountered on a vertical slice through the objects appearing on a plan. It is a two-dimensional, measured technical drawing showing the distances between these elements. Beginning with a simple line on the plan, a section is then projected upwards. A section shows only those elements that appear precisely on that line. A section does not show any depth or perspective. Sections are useful to verify that elements shown on a plan are in appropriate human scale, especially when people are included in the drawing. It can be particularly helpful to show a series of sections through a site in parallel, particularly where there is interesting or varied topography. The series builds up a

picture of the site in sequence, which can be very informative. A good landscape architectural section drawing will show elements not merely above ground, but also below.

SECTION ELEVATIONS

Section elevations, often simply called 'elevations', begin with exactly the same principles as a section drawing – with a line on the plan that is projected upwards. A section elevation, however, will show not only those elements that fall directly on the line, but everything appearing behind those elements looking in one direction. The apparent sizes of these objects do not shrink into the distance, as they would in a perspective drawing. They are pictured in exact scale regardless of their distance from the section line. Section elevations can provide a very complete image of a project, and are very useful for testing designs.

Section elevations
These section elevations by Lucy White help convey the experience of an elevated promenade that reinhabits an unused railway viaduct.

PERSPECTIVE

Perspective drawings are realistic, three-dimensional drawings that can do much to convey the feel, character and look of a site. Where orthographic projections are quantitative and measured drawings, perspectives are qualitative and unmeasured, allowing for much more emotional content and interpretation. Perspective drawings are constructed with imaginary lines that converge in the background in what is called a 'vanishing point'. These lines give the picture depth and often, a horizon.

Perspectives are extremely useful as a design tool, as they allow the designer to very quickly set a scene and evaluate human scale and impact. They are also very useful as a tool for selling a design. The general public is not always skilled at reading maps and plans, but will easily be able to comprehend information conveyed in a perspective drawing. The main drawback to perspective drawings is that they present a very static image, doing little to reflect the experience of moving through a site. As most sites are encountered by people in motion, this is a considerable liability.

Hand-drawn perspective (facing page)
A simple line drawing allows the designer to both test an idea and to communicate it.

Computer-rendered perspective (below)
Photorealistic visualisations can be a valuable aid for the designer seeking to sell a proposal to a client.

Axonometric drawing
This drawing for the Landschaftspark Duisburg-Nord allows the entire, complex, three-dimensional project to be comprehended in little more than a glance.

While perspective images are three-dimensional, it is rare that they are presented as scale or measured drawings. Axonometric projections are a relatively straightforward and convenient method of showing a site in three dimensions, as well as in accurate measure. Plans and sections have two axes: the x and y axes. Axonometric projections add in a third – the z axis. To create the projection, a plan image is rotated through a set number of degrees corresponding to the z axis, and the verticals are projected up from the plan to create a three-dimensional drawing that is precise.

Axonometric projections are often called 'bird's-eye views'. Like plan drawings, they place the viewer in an unnatural elevated position, which provides a feeling of power. As with plans, this can have negative consequences for the human qualities of a design. Axonometrics are still extremely useful, however, when used judiciously in combination with other types of representation.

AXONOMETRIC DRAWINGS

An axonometric drawing is a drawing created with a 45-degree angle between the x and z axes, which effectively tilts buildings up on to their bottom corners. It creates a slightly dizzy and uncomfortable angle for viewing. Axonometric drawings are also called 'military projections'.

ISOMETRIC DRAWINGS

Isometric drawings are created with a 30-degree angle between the x and z axes, tilting buildings up a bit more gently. Isometrics are very commonly used for communicating the site accurately and comfortably. There are two other axonometric projections: the dimetric and the trimetric. However, these are not commonly used in architectural drawings as they lose accuracy due to foreshortening.

MODELS

Models are a vital part of the design process, as they allow the designer to test ideas as actual built form without the expense and difficulty of building life-size prototypes. Models are useful at every stage of the design process, from initial site inventory and analysis to the presentation of the final design. In the early stages, contour models can be very useful as the landscape architect seeks to come to grips with the movement of water across the site, views, microclimates and a host of other considerations. Often, the initial model becomes a base for further explorations, with elements added and removed as requirements, thoughts or moods change. Models may be carefully measured to scale, or they may be rough approximations to test general ideas.

Models are constructed of a wide variety of materials. Topographic models are commonly constructed of wood, card or sheets of cork (attractive, but expensive). Wires are twisted into tree forms, buildings carved out of foam, or surface textures created with dustings of sand or shavings. The materials used for modelling are often used as reminders of what they represent, helping the designer to imagine the experience of the site. As models are usually created indoors, it is important to avoid using toxic materials or adhesives, especially as these cause pollution and illness in every stage of their manufacture and use. There is always a cleaner and cheaper alternative, and students are particularly resourceful in using reclaimed or recycled materials.

CONCEPTUAL MODELS

Conceptual models, like conceptual sketches, are used to explore ideas or relationships that are either encountered on the site or are proposed in the design. They may be used to generate a concept or metaphor that underpins the design, such as Kathryn Gustafson's scalloped shell design for Shell Petroleum's headquarters in France (see pages 78–79). Conceptual models often represent abstract ideas with materials that remind the designer of them – blue threads to represent the flow of water, perhaps, or fluffy cotton to show an area that is meant to be comfortable or happy. This practice helps the designer use intuitive processes as a lens on to the site. Designers, after all, are paid to daydream. The more real the model is to the designer, the more effectively their imaginations can take them to a design that fits the site.

Sketch model
This quickly constructed model allows the designer to explore qualities of light and shadow, enclosure and sequences, and to test human scale.

SKETCH MODELS

There is a limit to how much information drawings alone can provide, and it is often necessary to test an idea that has been developed in drawings as a prototype. Sketch models allow for ideas to be tested in a three-dimensional physical form, but without too much commitment to them. Sketch models are usually messy, and can often be downright ugly, but what is important is that they are a way to try things out. A sketch model that is beautifully executed and constructed can erroneously convince its creator that a concept is fully developed. Many a project has been stillborn in this way.

Sketch models are often used and reused, with elements added and torn away again, and the surface of the ground dug into and worked. Sketch models are very physical and can be deeply satisfying to create.

PRESENTATION MODELS

When at last a design is complete, and the time has come to present it to the client or the public for approval, a powerful communication and sales tool is required. This is the presentation model. Presentation models have an exceptionally high degree of finish, and they are time-consuming and often dizzyingly expensive to produce. They are scale models that provide not just an accurate representation of the design proposals, but also seek to imbue designs with additional glamour.

Presentation models, in landscape architecture in particular, are tricky to produce. Where a model of a building might seek to provide a scrupulously exact image of the finished product, a landscape presentation model finished in such a way runs the risk of looking like the setting for a miniature model train. It can be particularly challenging to choose materials to represent landscape that is sleek, sexy and contemporary.

Model of the Schouwburgplein, Rotterdam
West 8's presentation model for this celebrated design shows contemporary sensibilities and materials, restraint and elegance.

The Fundamentals of Landscape Architecture

COMPUTER-AIDED DESIGN (CAD)

Computer-Aided Design (CAD) has become a standard tool for designers in the space of only a few decades. It has added greatly to the range of available materials and methods for visualisation, while sometimes reducing the amount of time required to produce drawings. People often think of CAD as being composed of a few programs for creating highly technical engineering drawings, but in reality it is a vast range of programs that vary in complexity. As such, it includes not just the programs for engineering drawings, but programs for manipulating photographs, creating collages, creating diagrams and moving images. Outputs have kept pace with programs and we now have better equipment for visual display, with better, faster printers, including those that print three-dimensional prototypes.

While these programs and outputs are all incredibly useful, they are not ends unto themselves, but are simply parts of a designer's range of tools, which will always include working with physical materials and drawings, and of course, the faithful sketchbook.

ORTHOGRAPHIC PROJECTION

There are few, if any, landscape architecture firms left that do not create plans, sections and finished construction drawings using one of a handful of software applications created to assist with drafting. One of the original programs was AutoCAD. It is still a widely used program, along with MicroStation and Vectorworks. All these programs also include support for creating three-dimensional models. The chief advantage to these programs is their high degree of accuracy, which helps ensure that projects are built as they are envisioned. While setting up a drawing can still initially be laborious, once a base drawing is created, changes can be made quickly. This provides a great advantage over a hand-drawn plan, which must be completely redrawn for every change that occurs.

These programs are not intended to produce loose, natural-looking drawings in drafting applications, and finished presentation drawings are often retouched by hand or in other programs for manipulating graphics.

'Drawing has a much greater capacity for imaginative thought than is currently practised. Rarely are drawings understood and used as vehicles of creative thinking. Drawing is commonly taught as "graphic techniques" and "communications skills".'
James Corner

Photomontage
This image by Daphne Kao
self-consciously overlaps elements
so the techniques employed in
making the drawing are evident.

PHOTOMONTAGE

Photomontage and collage are techniques for bringing disparate elements together into an often photorealistic image. A number of computer programs exist to assist this process, including Adobe Photoshop and the open source program, Gimp. Photomontage creates bright and appealing perspective drawings, but it is also useful for retouching plans and sections created in drafting programs.

Computer photomontages can allow for both very realistic images to be created or for more loose and intuitive drawings, including sketches and conceptual drawings.

3D IMAGING

While drafting programs are capable of creating three-dimensional computer models, additional programs are available for a range of purposes and types of drawings. 3D models can be created relatively quickly, but without great accuracy, in applications such as SketchUp. More sophisticated graphics can be created in programs such as Rhino or 3ds Max. Outputs might vary from simple, blocky drawings that simply show topography and building masses to highly realistic models in which every leaf and window is pictured. In all of these programs, it is possible to create fly-throughs (or, perhaps more usefully, walk-throughs) showing the experience of spaces in the design in sequence, in just the way a person would experience the real design. Virtual reality also has the potential to function as an effective tool for architectural modelling.

STORYBOARDS

A journey on the Paris Metro (facing page)
Here, an underground trip is documented, showing a sequence of subterranean experiences directly related to a street map of the surface.

Making a motion picture or an animated sequence is a tremendously complicated and expensive procedure, and film directors or animators use a type of sketching technique to visualise the content of their film before the cameras roll. This is a process known as 'storyboarding', and it is very similar to the process of drawing a comic strip. A set of actions is shown incrementally, often in frames, rather than in the fluid movement that motion pictures provide. Because landscape architects design for fluid experiences and motion every bit as much as film-makers do, storyboarding can be an immensely useful way to imagine the way their design for a site will be used. It is also useful for communicating this experience to others.

Storyboards are, perhaps, under-used in landscape architecture, but they can be immensely instructive, particularly when showing the peripatetic experience – the walking experience – and when visualising complex sequences of urban spaces.

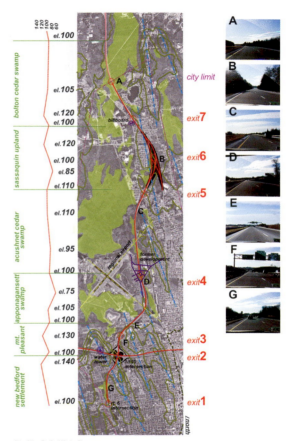

City of New Bedford Master Plan 012301
corridor analysis @ Rt.140

Highway corridor analysis (above)
The StoSS New Bedford Masterplan includes storyboarding as a technique for analysis. Photographs relate to a plan and graph, which allows a very complex story to be told with great economy of means.

THE MOVING IMAGE

Video technology and computer applications are making it much easier and cheaper to produce professional moving images. Design firms, especially landscape architectural firms, are profiting greatly from this access. Video is a superb communication tool that holds an audience transfixed. Advertisers are well aware of their persuasive power when their audience is gazing into a flickering light source. Selling the final design is only a small part of the power of the moving image for the landscape architect. The scope of the image, its ability to capture motion and its ability to capture changing moods and moments, create an almost ideal tool for examining the landscape. The motion and nuance of these images are a truer representation of the actual qualities of the landscape.

As with any medium, it has limitations, and in the case of the moving image it is the ability of these images to mesmerise that is a failing. The hypnotic effect of moving images can also work on the designer.

Animation in landscape architectural representation presents the possibility of creating a moving photomontage, a landscape that is populated with the products of the designer's imagination. There is an almost limitless combination of possibilities, including mixing live action with animation. When combined with other possibilities, such as panoramic video and virtual reality, animated video has incredible potential.

Tindal Square, Chelmsford, in movement
This student project from the Writtle School of Design allows a complex analysis of motion, activity and occupation of public space at different times of day and on different days of the week. The technique could certainly also be extended to include seasons.

RELAXING

time

EATING

Saracens
Bar & Eaterie
Every
MON & THURS
COCKTAILS
2 for 1
from
7pm

POINT 1 00:00:06

SATURDAY SUNDAY

WEDNESDAY FRIDAY

SHOPPING

00:00:02:12

SLOW YOUR PACE

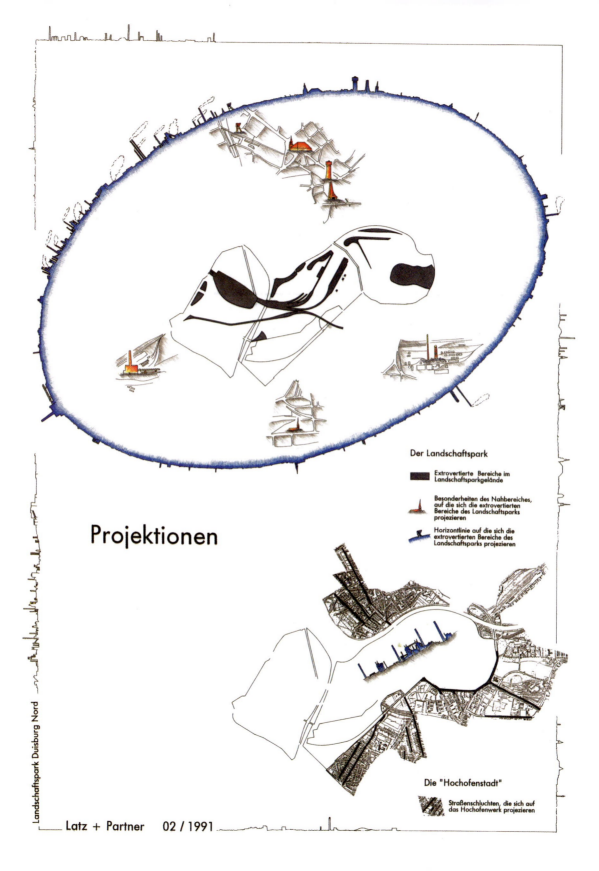

Der Landschaftspark

Extrovertierte Bereiche im Landschaftsparkgelände

Besonderheiten des Nahbereiches, auf die sich die extrovertierten Bereiche des Landschaftsparks projezieren

Horizontlinie auf die sich die extrovertierten Bereiche des Landschaftsparks projezieren

Projektionen

Die "Hochofenstadt"

Straßenschluchten, die sich auf das Hochofenwerk projizieren

Landschaftspark Duisburg Nord

Latz + Partner   02 / 1991

PRESENTATION

Landscape architects must have skill in presenting complex issues and their solutions in a simple, straightforward way. They often deal with audiences with a wide variety of skills and levels of understanding, and often, presentation materials must be made to work for all these audiences. Presentations involve a combination of the printed word, the spoken word and images. A very standard format might include a couple of large, board-mounted, printed boards, arranged on easels; a computer slide presentation; and a site model. Presentations may be made at many stages throughout the design process, first when a firm is bidding for a job and showing their skills and experience, and then as designs are developed, communicating with the clients and in public consultation. Later in the design process, finished design proposals may be presented to clients and the general public,

which may be presented and published in a variety of ways in a variety of media.

Books and pamphlets play an important part in design presentation as well, and landscape architects often gain substantial skills as graphic designers, as they create completed studies and proposals in book form.

Landscape architectural education generally includes many opportunities to hone presentation skills and to gain confidence.

Presentation board, 'Philadelphia's Catalysts' (left)
This competition poster allows a complicated message to be communicated on a single sheet, without the benefit of the designer's presence to explain the content in person. A board produced as an aid to a verbal presentation would generally be much less reliant on text.

Presentation board, Landschaftspark Duisburg-Nord (facing page)
Compelling imagery and masterful page layout are helpful in promoting a project at the presentation stage.

THE PORTFOLIO

The design portfolio is a very specific type of presentation, intended to convey the skills and experience of an individual designer to a specific audience. Every student of landscape architecture leaves their university studies with a portfolio of work that supports them in selling their services for employment. Designers keep their portfolios refreshed and up to date throughout the course of their careers. The portfolio is a designed presentation that generally has a printed format. It can also be produced in a digital or web format, sometimes solely so. The samples of work included in a portfolio are intended to display the range of a designer's capabilities, showing drawings in various media and using various computer applications. Often the portfolio must speak for itself in the absence of the designer, and thus, it is important to have carefully written text to tie the images together. Text is particularly useful for showing a designer's work process – how they achieved a design solution – as it is important for a prospective employer to see and evaluate where their skills will best be used.

The array of drawing skills, media, text and imagery that are included in the portfolio are far more than just a job application or curriculum vitae. They literally paint a picture of a person's ability and the range of knowledge they acquire in a very holistic field. The portfolio is an image of the designer's identity, and as such, a source of pride.

A page from a student portfolio
Combining text and images with clarity is of paramount importance in preparing a successful portfolio. This uncluttered page communicates the designer's proficiency with model building and his ability to articulate what those models were intended to achieve.

Model Making

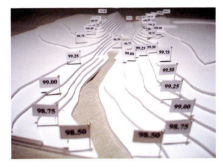

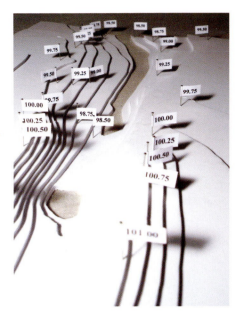

Writtle College Grounds Assignment:
Part of the Redesign involved cut and fill excavation where
calculations were required for the final build

Contextual Models of both Topography and Context:
The models show my final comprehensive design project of the
former Gasworks site, Chelmsford, Essex
Implications for ground modelling design and potential flooding
hazards are identified

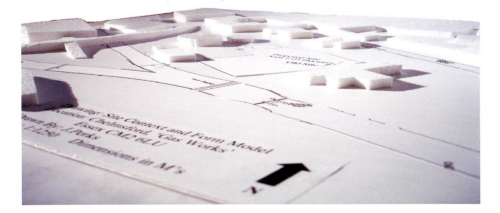

The Fundamentals of Landscape Architecture

5

THE ANATOMY OF A PROJECT

So many variables have to be taken into account in a project that it can seem mystifyingly complex when explained, especially since the design process is both subjective and objective. It is all relatively straightforward, though, when a project is seen as a sequence from beginning to end. This chapter takes the opportunity to present a single project as a case study. The designs and masterplan for four unique public spaces in Coventry, England, provide a very good window on how a design team is assembled, how a concept blossoms into a design, and how the final design is realised.

Rummey Design, Millennium Place, Coventry, England
This curving wall is the product of a collaboration between the designers and the artist Jochen Gerz.

THE COVENTRY PHOENIX INITIATIVE

'The scheme is driven by public space, not conventional architecture.'
Hugh Pearman

Coventry is a city in the heart of England, roughly halfway between London and Manchester. As with many cities in England's Midlands, it experienced explosive growth during the Industrial Revolution and became a busy and thriving manufacturing town – in particular, the manufacture of cars, motors, watches and clocks. It began as a base for the Church in the Middle Ages, and has been an important ecclesiastical centre since then.

Coventry suffered intensive firebombing during the Second World War, which obliterated much of its historic core, including its fine cathedral. However, the city fared well in a post-war boom with a resurgence in manufacturing. Sir Basil Spence's elegant and austere Coventry Cathedral was opened in 1962, adjacent to the ruins of the old cathedral. Spence envisioned Coventry Cathedral as a phoenix rising from the ashes of war. While his cathedral remains a noble work of architecture, it stood in the undignified surroundings of ugly buildings hastily built to accommodate the economic boom. In a sense, Coventry was blitzed twice. First by the Luftwaffe, and secondly by eager developers. Economic decline through the 1970s and 1980s saw these buildings become stark symbols on a beleaguered skyline.

Coventry's urban fabric was desperately in need of re-stitching, and thus the Phoenix Initiative was launched to repair the ravages of two blitzes. First, by focusing on the public realm, exterior urban spaces and the life within them; secondly, by working on the buildings; and thirdly, by reconnecting the city (the hinterland had become disconnected, for pedestrians, from the centre). Landscape architects and urban designers, Rummey Design, worked with architects MacCormac Jamieson Prichard (MJP), among many other collaborators to effect this repair. This project was selected for inclusion in this book because of its impressive range. It is an urban itinerary – a number of spaces, each a fine place with unique character, strung together to make a compelling story. It weaves landscape, urbanism, art, planning, transportation, archaeology and history together on the warp and weft of ambition and hope.

The view from Priory Place, Coventry
The vista from Priory Place towards Millennium Place at the Coventry Phoenix Initiative highlights some of the issues encountered on the site. From this view, the strong change in elevation across the site is highlighted, as only the top of the Whittle Arch at Millennium Place is visible. This view, taken at dusk, also shows how the careful lighting design allows a seamless transition from day to night, allowing for lively inhabitation across a broad time span every day.

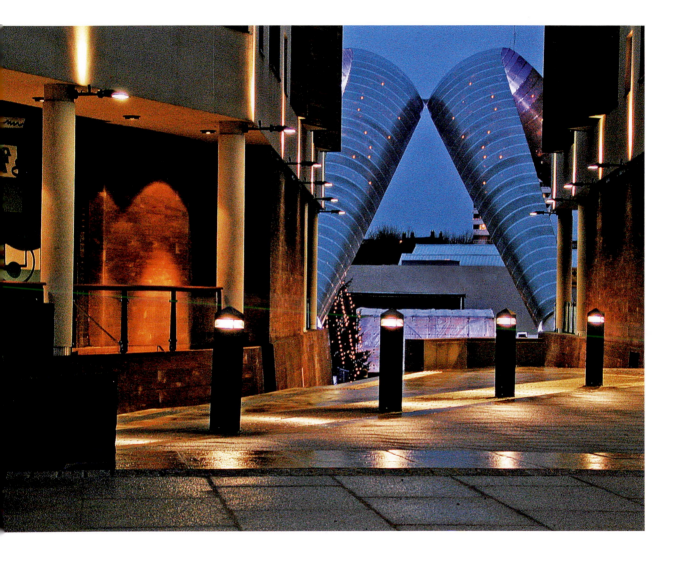

THE PROJECT TIMELINE

Projects in landscape architecture progress through stages, from the very first contact with the client and awareness of the site, through to the realisation, construction and maturation of the finished design. It's important to remember that the design process, unlike a timeline, is often completely non-linear. The phrase 'back to the drawing board' refers to the continual process of testing and retesting that is characteristic of the architectures. The rest of this chapter will follow this timeline, explaining each stage in further detail.

1. BRIEF

2. CONCEPT

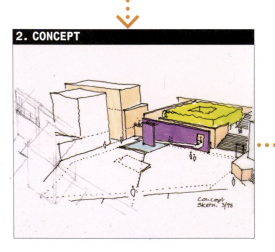

3. ANALYSIS

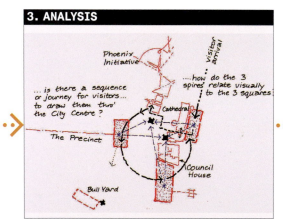

4. SYNTHESIS

5. DETAIL DEVELOPMENT

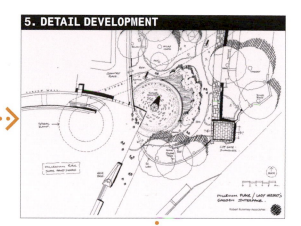

7. MATURATION

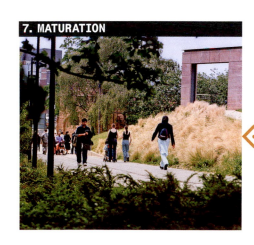

6. CONSTRUCTION

1. BRIEF

The brief is the initial description of the project problem that defines the parameters within which the designer will work. It is presented initially to invite bids for projects from design firms. It then forms the basis for the work once a suitable firm is selected. The brief outlines the history of a site and the client's aspirations for it. It also includes the discussion of any constraints to design. The project budget and timescale are established, along with a description of the composition of the project team.

At Coventry, there were two clients: the Coventry City Council and the Millennium Commission. Their brief sought quality urban design for living, while combining landscape and urban design, public art and architecture as a way of regenerating the centre. There was also the desire to create a spectacle that would serve as a symbol both for Coventry's regeneration and for a new millennium. Uniting and connecting key urban elements within the city centre across the city's topography was also an aim, along with creating an awareness of both the past and the future.

Some early priorities that emerged for the project were the demolition of large parking structures and the closure of a major traffic interchange to eliminate physical barriers to the regeneration, both physical and cultural, of Coventry's city centre.

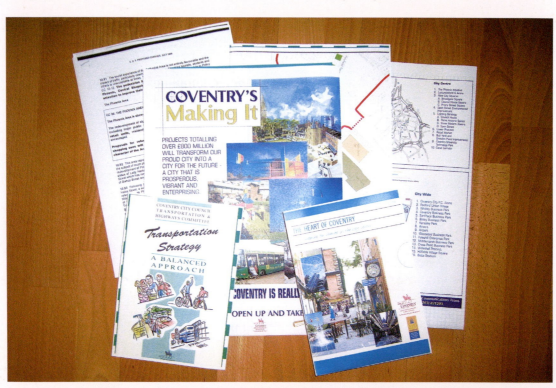

A range of documents supporting the Coventry brief
The brief often follows on from a wider body of strategic work that both sets the context and establishes the need for a project. Coventry had been the subject of numerous studies and strategies that all pointed to the need for regeneration at the city's centre.

CONTRIBUTORS TO THE PHOENIX INITIATIVE

The client
Coventry City Council and the Millennium Commission were the two clients for the project. Together they wrote the brief and provided oversight for the project throughout.

Surveyors
Surveyors are employed to take important measurements throughout the project. They measure the site and any buildings, levels and topography. Surveyors may also be employed to measure costs and the timescale for the project.

Architects
MacCormac Jamieson Prichard worked closely with Rummey Design to realise the project and to ensure that buildings were in tune with Coventry's landscape. They were responsible for designing the buildings and the site's Millennium arch – the Whittle Arch.

Artists
Several artists were involved with the project at almost every stage, and major artworks were included in every part of the designs. Artworks were intended to be integral to the site, not merely objects placed in the landscape.

Engineers
Different types of engineers, including structural, mechanical and electrical engineers, from firms such as Whitbybird, were employed in various phases of the projects, from building design to lighting.

Accounting and legal
Accounting and legal services are fundamental to ensuring that a project stays on track from inception to construction.

Stakeholders
Literally, a stakeholder is anyone who stands to gain from, or has a benevolent interest in, a given project. The Phoenix Initiative was supported by the East Midlands Development Agency (EMDA), the Millennium Commission and CDP – a private developer that built apartments on the site. The local community is always an important stakeholder.

Lighting designers
Although many landscape architects are skilled with lighting design, the complexities of the Phoenix Initiative required the involvement of a specialist lighting firm, Speirs and Major.

Contractors
All the planning and designing must eventually become a built thing, and the contractors take the plans and make them a built reality. Skilled, experienced and conscientious contractors are essential.

CONTRIBUTORS AND THEIR ROLES
Because of the broad interdisciplinary range of landscape architecture, landscape architects are often ideal communicators, working at the heart of project teams to ensure a holistic view is taken throughout. It is essential to maintain good communication and working relations between members of the team to ensure that each plays their part at the correct time and in the most productive manner. The Coventry Phoenix Initiative involved a particularly large and varied team, although it could also have included environmental assessors, interior architects and tourism consultants, among others.

The Fundamentals of Landscape Architecture

2. CONCEPT

In an urban landscape with mournful associations, it is important to make peace with the past in order to move into the future. This was the poignant case presented by Coventry's city centre, which bore the scars of violence and inept and radical surgery. Time, memory, reconciliation and citizenship were all seen as central themes that would underlie the concept. It was important to foster communication in the public spaces, to bring them to life with all their historic associations: war and destruction, the Church and its buildings, industry, and the ceaseless movement of people and goods.

Rummey Design developed a concept that would provide a journey through Coventry's past, present and future. The route begins at the Priory Garden, where archaeology and the cloisters provide an immediate link to 1,000 years of history. The Millennium Gate at the city centre, now marked by the Whittle Arch, signifies the present and a future of optimism and cooperation. It is also posited at the end by the Garden of International Friendship.

The concept provided a framework for understanding each site in the context of a progression, providing cues for design. Further, it allowed a simple and elegant logic to be applied to the site, which artists could work within and the general public could grasp in an instant. Concepts need not be elaborate in any way. In fact, a refined message, such as that at Coventry, is usually most easily digested and yields the most satisfying results for all.

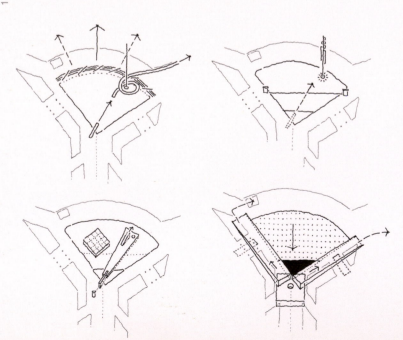

Sketch proposals for Millennium Place
Proposals exploring the theme of time were projected onto the space of Millennium Place during the process of developing the concept.

The journey

The concept eventually came to represent a journey through time from Coventry's past to its future, through the various spaces of the Phoenix Initiative. This diagram of the journey proved an exceptionally useful tool for explaining the concept, not only to the client, stakeholders and the general public, but for communicating with other collaborators in the design such as the artists and the lighting designers.

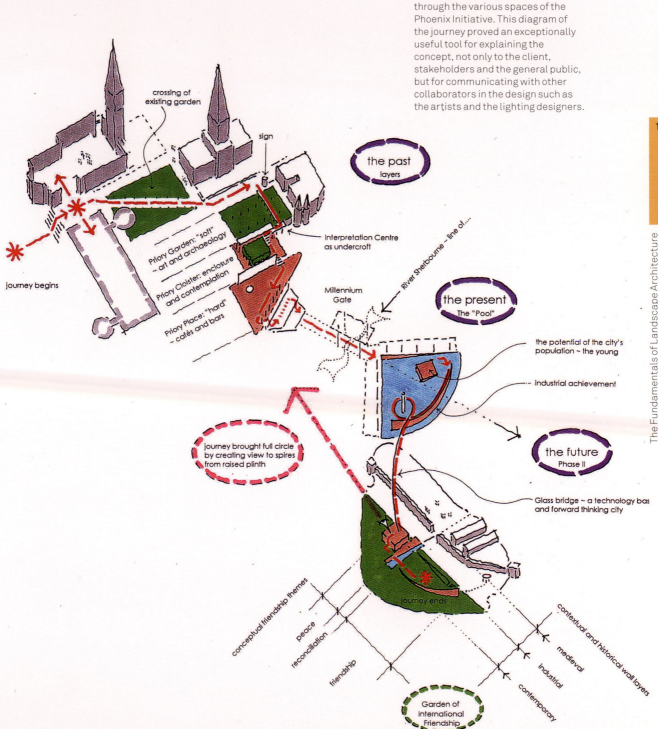

crossing of
existing garden

sign

the past
layers

journey begins

Priory Garden: "soft"
~ art and archaeology

Priory Cloister: enclosure
and contemplation

Priory Place: "hard"
~ cafés and bars

Interpretation Centre
as undercroft

Millennium
Gate

River Sherbourne ~ line of...

the present
The "Pool"

the potential of the city's
population ~ the young

industrial achievement

journey brought full circle
by creating view to spires
from raised plinth

the future
Phase II

Glass bridge ~ a technology base
and forward thinking city

conceptual friendship themes

peace

reconciliation

friendship

journey ends

contextual and historical wall layers

medieval

industrial

contemporary

Garden of
International
Friendship

3. ANALYSIS

Coventry was seen to have the possibility to be a 'city of the future' – a bold, modern city filled with whizzing cars and smart buildings. One of the earliest ring roads was built around Coventry's city centre with the hope of speeding circulation. Effectively, though, this road simply served to strangle the centre by separating it from its hinterlands. The ring road, and transportation in general, was at the forefront of the site analysis. Providing a traffic-free progression of pedestrian spaces was a primary objective, and the site was marred by a major intersection and an antiquated and ill-designed bus station. Further, as the design progressed it became obvious this already constrained site would have to accept the existing Sainsbury's supermarket as it was, without modification.

Archaeology also proved to be a key consideration, as the site had been occupied for over 1,000 years; layer upon significant layer of civilisation lay beneath the surface. Careful coordination was required among the design team, George Demidowicz – the city archaeologist, English Heritage, and Chris Beck, the project director. In the course of the investigations, the BBC television programme *Time Team* covered the emerging archaeology as the works progressed.

Analysis drawing, Priory Garden, Coventry
The analysis for the Priory Garden required careful consideration of the archaeological remains present on the site. This layered drawing of the site begins to draw out cues for design as well as to identify areas where cautious excavation is required.

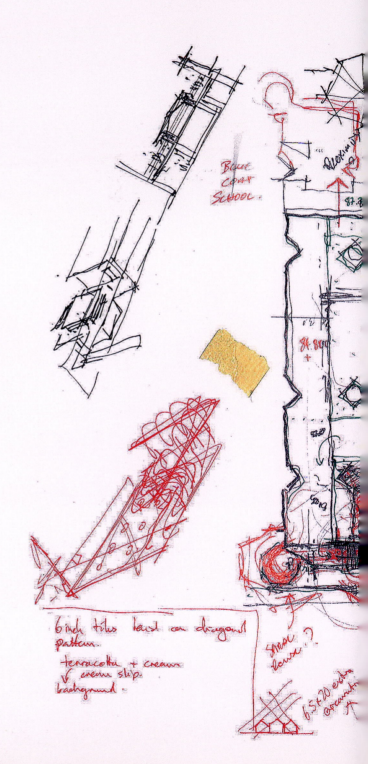

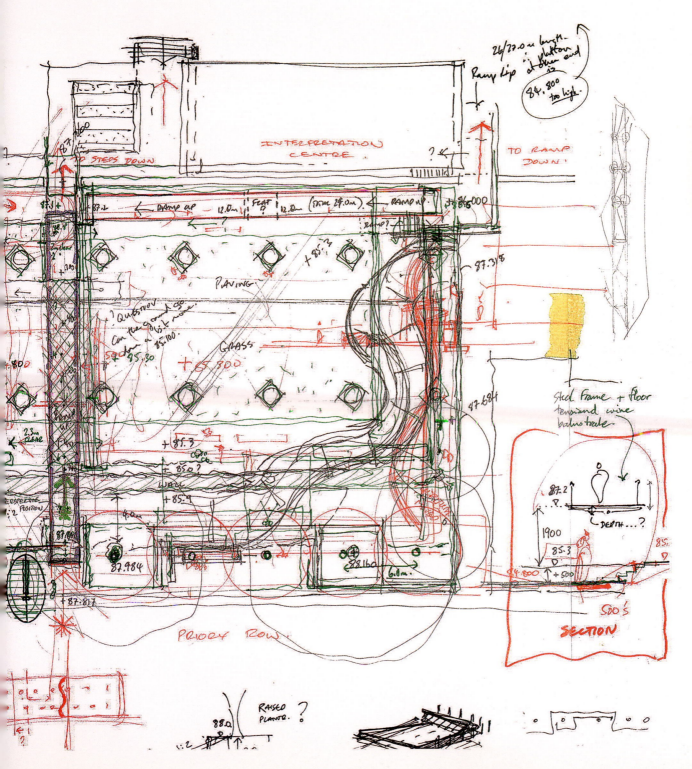

4. SYNTHESIS

'Only a fool will build in defiance of the past. What is new and significant always must be grafted to old roots.'
Béla Bartók

In design, synthesis is the process of bringing analysis and ideas together to create design solutions for the problems that are posed by the brief. The design process supports this synthesis by allowing numerous possibilities to be tested. This can be an extremely wide-ranging process, but the design concept is useful to keep the explorations within certain bounds. For the Coventry Phoenix Initiative, the concept of moving on a trajectory through the past, present and future informed all stages of the design synthesis, and provided a strong focus for all the different contributors to the process, including the significant number of artists involved.

As a case in point, the artist Susanna Heron's sculpture, *Waterwindow*, is seamlessly integrated into the landscape design. It provides an aperture through the wall that divides Priory Garden from Priory Place, two of the scheme's linked spaces. It is a square cut in the wall behind a waterfall. Through this window, visitors moving from the 'past' may glimpse the 'future' spaces ahead of them. This view is veiled and framed as a vista, which provides a hint of the future. And, meaningfully, what is new and significant is 'grafted to old roots'.

'Threshold Wall' concept sketches
The design for the *Waterwindow* began as a series of explorations of the threshold between two important spaces within the design. The steep slope across the site separated the two spaces. Above is the Priory Cloister, a quiet, contemplative space that reflects the site's ecclesiastical heritage. Below is Priory Place, bordered by restaurants and new offices for the BBC. Making the transition between the two spaces required a decisive move that was eventually to become the *Waterwindow*.

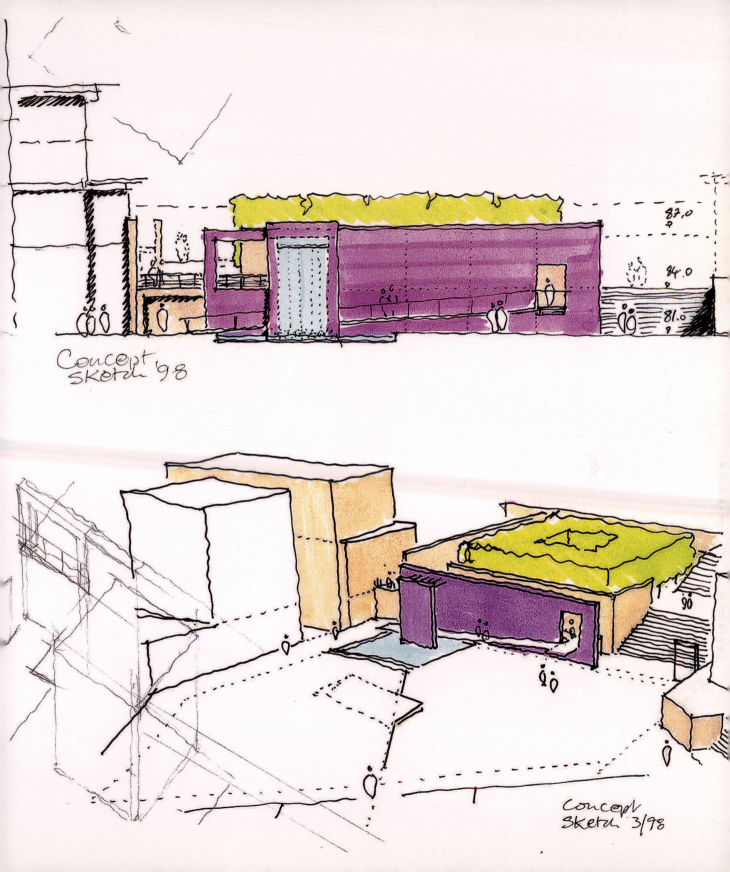

Concept
Sketch '98

Concept
Sketch 3/98

87.0

84.0

81.0

90

Diagramming the Threshold Wall

Annotated diagrams allowed further exploration of the transition between the Priory Cloister and Priory Place. There is much complexity to making such a transition, first because of the issues raised by negotiating the change in levels and all the possible ways in which to do so, and secondly because of the interplay between materials, water, and the human experience. Diagrams and sketches allow the designer to envision the experience. It is the crucial link between drawing and the imagination that allows the designer to test ideas in advance. A designer is able to 'feel' the experience with the same vividness that a musician can 'hear' melody and orchestration from printed sheet music.

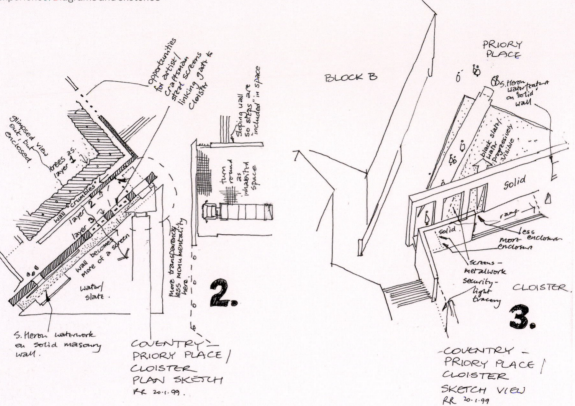

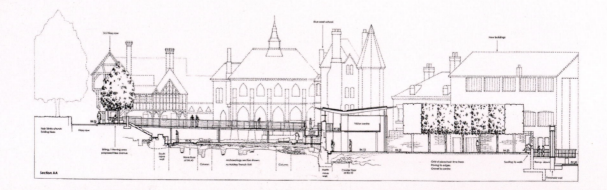

Axonometric sketch for the Priory Quarter

As the designs evolve, they become more tangible and the drawings become more detailed. This annotated sketch is clarifying a wide range of design questions across three distinct areas of the site, including Priory Place and the Priory Cloister. Further changes in level are addressed with ramps and stairways, and details of plants and surfaces are all beginning to coalesce. The comprehensive nature of this drawing might seem to indicate that the details gelled quickly, but this drawing would have been supported by countless quick sketches, and certainly would have been followed by countless more.

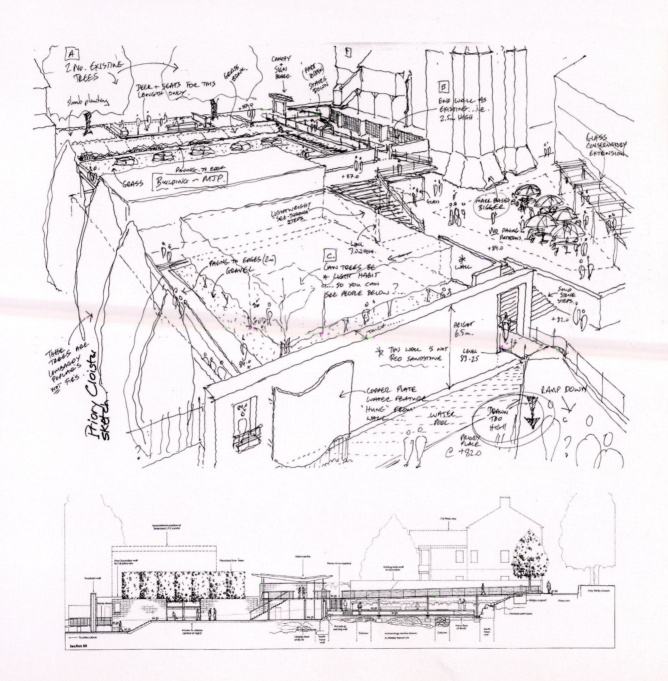

Coventry Phoenix Initiative Plan (facing page)

When at last all the complex details are worked out, the whole project may be presented as a plan. Priory Cloister appears at the centre of the lower half of the drawing, and is recognisable as a small grid of trees. Just above, at the centre of the drawing is Priory Place, which takes the form of two triangles to either side of a diagonal axis. The buildings around Priory Place form an arrow point in plan where the Whittle Arch launches across the road and into fan-shaped Millennium Place, which represents Coventry's bustling present. From there, a glass walkway spirals off into 'the future', arching above Coventry's historic city wall.

The completed *Waterwindow* at Priory Place (above)

The completed project owes a clear debt to the early concept drawings, but it is clear to see how much the idea evolved. Careful choices of materials, including stone, wood, steel, copper, and, of course, water, complement each other in a bold interplay of colour and texture.

The ramp to the right prolongs the transition from the Priory Cloister, which is behind the wall, and provides a courtly entrance into the hubbub of Priory Place. Like actors peering from the wings, visitors to the space can size up the action in Priory Place from behind the *Waterwindow* before they make their appearance.

5. DETAIL DEVELOPMENT

After the draft plans for the Coventry Phoenix Initiative had been approved by the clients, Rummey Design and the rest of the design team kicked into high gear to finalise the designs and to produce the measured drawings from which the scheme would be constructed. Detail drawings include a wide range of considerations, including paving, planting, street furniture, lighting, grading and drainage. Sets of drawings were created for each discrete space within the scheme and these drawings were then issued to the contractors so that construction could begin.

Paving detail (facing page)
This drawing includes both a plan and a section to indicate materials used on surfaces in Millennium Place. The drawing incorporates photographs as well as descriptions of the materials for absolute clarity. Note that the section includes people and vehicles, again to provide scale.

Priory Quarter axonometric (left, above)
A site as complex as the Coventry Phoenix Initiative requires a vast number of drawings of all different types. The detail drawings are, in many ways, just like the directions that might come with a model or a piece of flat-pack furniture. They are, however, very much more prescriptive in specifying exact measurements and methods of construction. This axonometric drawing would help the contractor to understand the total context and construction for this area of the site, and help to provide reference points for further drawings showing closer details.

Detail for a vitrine in the Priory Garden (left, below)
Archaeological details in the Priory Garden are highlighted and celebrated with vitrines – glass display cases. This detail shows the materials and methods of construction as well as the intended relationship between the viewers and the vitrines. Measurements are shown with dimension lines, but the inclusion of people in the image helps to establish scale and thus safeguard against any errors.

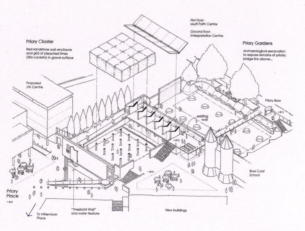

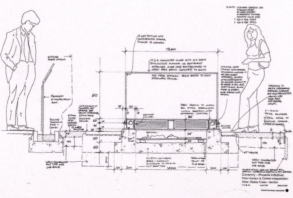

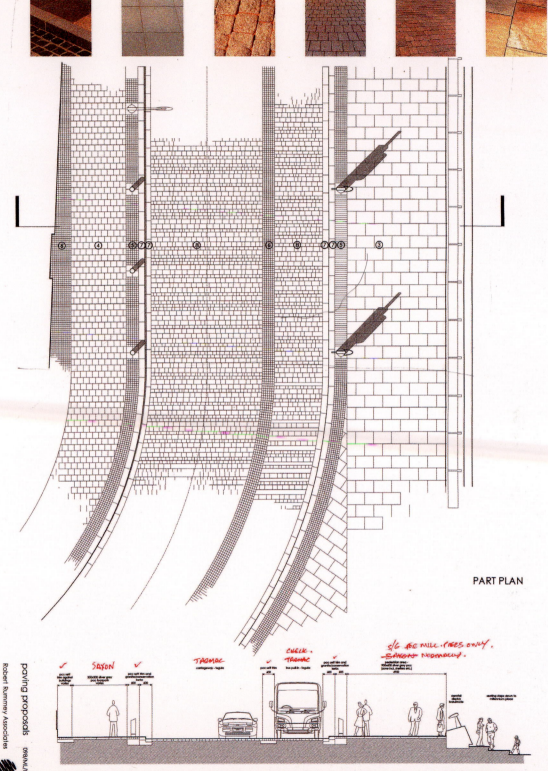

PART PLAN

paving proposals

Robert Rummey Associates

098/IML/005

SAXON

TARMAC

CHALK.
TARMAC

TYPICAL SECTION

6. CONSTRUCTION

The Threshold Wall at Priory Place
The finishes are beginning to be applied in this image. The concrete core for the wall in which the *Waterwindow* will appear is complete, and paving stones sit in the foreground awaiting installation. The lone workman on his tea break at the centre of the photograph will presumably be joined by a much larger team later!

After the hard work involved in producing the detail drawings, it is immensely gratifying to the landscape architect to witness the breaking of ground on the site. However, the construction process is also fraught with anxiety as the landscape architect must supervise the work throughout the construction process, ensuring that materials and finishes are as specified and that workmanship is of a consistently high standard. The finished quality of the construction often reflects on the landscape architect as much as it does on the contractor. Therefore, it is crucial to ensure that the job is well done.

Throughout the process of construction, the landscape architect remains in contact with the design team and the contractors, signing off the work at every stage of completion.

Laying paving at Priory Place
Stone pavers are set into a bed of levelled sand, which provides a flexible and resilient surface that resists cracking and heaving.

Applying finishes to the *Waterwindow*

The *Waterwindow* can be seen taking shape. Here the workman is standing on the edge of what will become the pond below the waterfall. The wall itself is covered with bright new copper, still covered in protective sheeting. Once the sheeting is removed, the copper will quickly acquire its characteristic green verdigris patina, which will provide a soft, muted backdrop for the waterfall.

7. MATURATION

From the time a building is constructed, it begins to age and deteriorate. One of the great joys of landscape architecture is that the landscape architect does not witness a single moment of perfection. A process, rather, is set in motion. The site, now built and planted, slowly fills out, grows and takes on life and occupation. Needless to say, much can go wrong in this process, and often, inadequate maintenance is to blame. However, if a work of landscape architecture is properly cared for and maintained, it will grow and mature as a community asset for many times the lifetime of the designer. Some of the great works of the past, such as Central Park and the Champs Elysées, have continued to develop and add value for their entire existences, and should do so for many years to come. The Coventry Phoenix Initiative has added significant value to Coventry's city centre, injecting new community life as well as economic life into the area. It is certain that the project's long-term legacy to Coventry will be of great benefit for many, many years into the future.

The majestically lit bridge and arch at Millennium Place, Coventry
Modular construction again allows for individual pieces to be replaced in the event of damage, and individual elements are durable enough to withstand long use over considerable time. Other areas of the site are less urban and hard-edged, with plants and trees that, over time, will continue to grow and improve. The legacy of the improved value of the area and the reinvigoration of Coventry's city centre are priceless assets that will continue to produce over time.

Susanna Heron's *Waterwindow* at Priory Place, Coventry
This photo of the completed site shows how comfortably the crisp, contemporary look and finish of the design fits with its historic backdrop. Here the copper backdrop to the *Waterwindow* has acquired its green patina as the copper comes into contact with the air and water. The site has, as we say, 'good bones', meaning that its structure is carefully considered and successful. As paving slabs break or benches are vandalised, replacement and maintenance can be easily accomplished because the vision for the site has created such a clear framework.

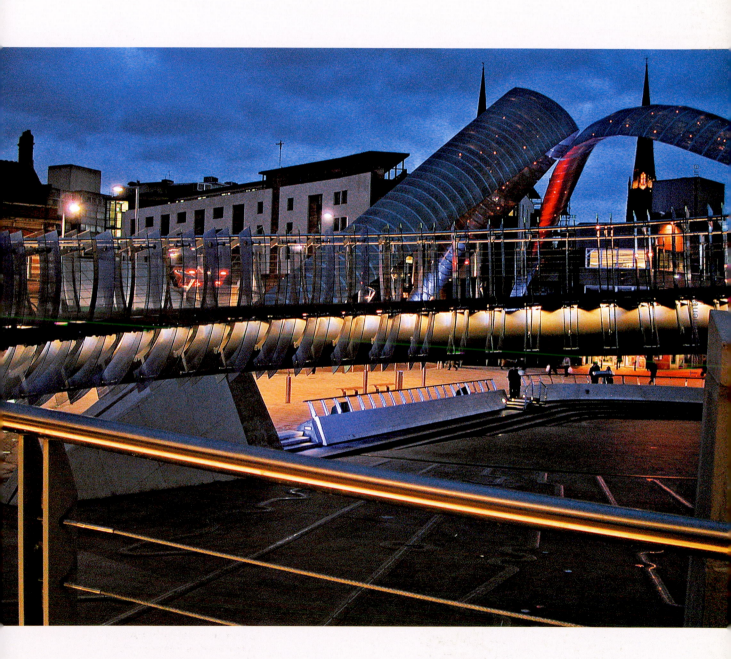

6

CAREERS

This chapter sets out a few of the general areas in which landscape architects are employed, to show both the great scope of the field and the possibility for specialising within the profession.

There are few clearly defined career paths in landscape architecture, which can be both a blessing and a curse. Landscape architects will often, in the course of an average work week, spend time working as a landscape manager, project manager, designer, landscape planner, and urban designer, among many other possibilities. This can create an immensely rich, varied and interesting working life.

Landscape architecture has tremendous potential to envision and craft a better future for people and the planet, and skilled, creative and open-minded people are needed to help secure it.

Mary Miss, Jyvaskyla University, 1994
A temporary landscape installation that captures the essence of the Finnish pine forest.

DESIGN AND VISION

Packaging up the big picture – a vision – for a project is central to the work of nearly all landscape architects. Strong visual and verbal communication skills are essential to convey the essence of a proposal to a client, but they are also an indispensable aid to the design process. Design involves using word and image to think imaginatively through all the many variables that may be found on or around a site to reach a design conclusion. This is important for the individual designer, but the ability to think and represent ideas on the fly is crucial for a landscape architect working as part of a team.

Design begins with researching, analysing and understanding a site. From here, a unique concept or strategy is crafted into a proposal for its development or improvement. The proposal is then presented to the client and often to the general public. Computer visualisation is probably the most common form of representation in offices today, and CAD programmes such as AutoCAD, MicroStation and SketchUp are used heavily. Graphics-editing programmes, such as Photoshop or Gimp, are also very useful for creating photorealistic depictions of a design. Animation, video and 3D visualisations are also effective and visually exciting methods of communicating a design.

Jacques Wirtz, Cogels Park, Schoten, 1977

Cogels Park was an early project of the firm Wirtz International, and its design elements are classic, even timeless. This small park was formerly the grounds of a private home, and the design of the park is intended to feel private, personal and intimate. The park is surrounded by mature plantings, which reinforce the sense of seclusion and enclosure. Curving paths, placid ponds and plantings of trees and shrubs accentuate a sequence of movement through the park. The organic flow of movement through the park is punctuated with enigmatic pyramids of cobblestones and ivy, whose crisp, clean figures provide formal contrast.

Cogels Park is an eloquent example of the fact that great landscape design does not need to be assertive or emblematic to be successful. Cogels Park, as an enduring design, is a legacy to its community.

PLANNING THE LANDSCAPE

Landscape planning is the art of balancing existing and desired land uses for an area, and also suggesting alternative uses. Specialisation is desirable in professions such as traffic management and building, but landscape planners must be skilled generalists, bringing strong knowledge of many areas together to make holistic solutions. To a specialist, land use might seem very straightforward and possible to represent with blocks of colour drawn on a plan. To a landscape planner, any site, no matter how small or large, peels apart layer after interdependent layer. One landscape, for example, might be expected to provide space for housing, flood control, animal habitat, transportation and industry.

Landscape planning today owes a great debt to the ideas of the American landscape architect Ian McHarg, whose 1969 book, *Design with Nature*, set out with great clarity the methods of analysing the landscape in just these sorts of layers. McHarg's ideas and methods have now matured into Geographic Information Systems (GIS), computer-based ecological and land analysis, which has revolutionised land-use planning.

Landscape planners are typically concerned with natural and built environments over large areas such as park systems, transportation networks, agricultural areas or geographic regions. Corridors are also commonly studied or designed, and these might include transportation corridors such as roads and canals, greenways or wildlife migration routes. Environmental reclamation or remediation is often at the centre of such projects, and landscape planners are commonly employed on sites such as mining landscapes or wetland ecosystems.

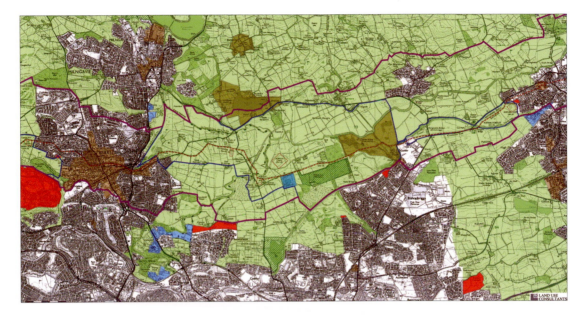

Land Use Consultants, Antonine Wall, Scotland

Many people will be familiar with the Roman fortification of Hadrian's Wall, built to separate Roman-occupied territory from the untamed area that is now Scotland. A second fortification, the Antonine Wall, was built between the Forth and the Clyde in the 2nd Century. As part of the process for applying for World Heritage status, Land Use Consultants (LUC) conducted a study to identify a buffer zone around the site to protect the landscape around the wall. Linear features such as the Antonine Wall form powerful tools for protecting and managing large swathes of landscape, and LUC developed new methods during this unique project to do so. GIS studies formed the basis for the research, in particular to analyse views to and from the wall. Both natural and artificial boundaries, formed by topography or urban development, formed a framework for ranking the importance of areas and determining the size and shape of the buffer zone.

MANAGEMENT AND CONSERVATION

'It is time to employ one of the greatest human talents, the ability to manipulate the environment that has become hostile to life itself into a humane habitat which sustains life and nurtures growth, both personal and collective.'
Anne Whiston Spirn

Landscape planning and landscape management and conservation are often one and the same thing. A landscape planner, for example, might create a landscape management plan for an area after the planning work has balanced the land use requirements. It differs, though, in that it involves working with designed landscapes to ensure that they mature in the way that was intended by the designer. Landscape management also ensures that landscapes maintain optimum ecological health, supporting the maximum possible biodiversity.

Landscape management assumes that a landscape is an environmental, social, cultural and economic resource. As such, landscapes need protection and conservation to maintain their vitality and productivity in all these areas. Protection and conservation is never passive, however, so landscape architects develop policies and actions to accomplish this.

Landscape management, as with all facets of landscape architecture, is a fundamentally interdisciplinary undertaking, involving a wide range of professions, including architects, archaeologist, hydrologists, surveyors and botanists to name a few. Landscape managers are often employed to have responsibility for urban or national parks, nature reserves or industrial landscapes.

Iguazu Falls, Argentina
Protecting a valuable natural resource such as Iguazu Falls is often greatly helped by income from tourism. This creates issues in itself, though, as the impact of large numbers of visitors upon a site can be devastating to beauty, wilderness and biodiversity. Balancing these factors is often the work of landscape managers.

HISTORIC CONSERVATION

The grounds of stately homes and celebrated gardens might immediately spring to mind where historic landscape conservation is concerned, but this is only a small part of the picture. The great variety of cultural landscapes that have been granted UNESCO World Heritage status gives some indication of the scope of historic conservation. A cursory glance at the list of World Heritage sites turns up the wet tropics of Queensland, the walled city of Baku, the valley of the Loire River in France, and the ancient city of Machu Picchu.

As with landscape planning, management and conservation, the work involved in historic landscape conservation is fundamentally interdisciplinary, involving collaboration with a range of professionals which may include architects, archaeologists (including garden archaeologists), and probably a few librarians and archivists along the way as well.

Taj Mahal Cultural Heritage District Development Plan

The Taj Mahal Cultural Heritage District Development Plan shows that the work of historic conservation is often much more than merely defending valued heritage sites from environmental or other degradation. This project involves the planning and design of a riverfront park and promenade that would serve to complement and provide a setting for the Taj Mahal and the nearby Agra Fort. The park would also provide a productive landscape that would help absorb some of the impact of tourism while providing recreational opportunities for the local community.

The park's riverfront promenade will provide an important physical and visual link between the two monuments, expanding the range of tourism beyond the Taj Mahal to the Fort, enriching the experience for visitors while serving as a pressure valve for the high numbers that come to the Taj Mahal. The park would also help highlight the area's other assets, including additional Mughal tombs and the remains of recently excavated pleasure gardens in the area. Finally, interpreting the heritage is an important part of the project, from providing displays and signage to designing tourist itineraries through the sites. Much of the work of conservation involves making heritage visible so that it can be appreciated and cherished. Conservation work involves not just landscape and built form, but the popular imagination as well. Pictured are the Taj Mahal and Agra Fort.

THE SCIENCE OF LANDSCAPE

The scientific processes that shape the landscape are of great importance to landscape architects, and there is often significant overlap between landscape architecture and landscape or environmental science. It is relatively common for individuals with a first degree in environmental science or a related field to round out their qualification with an additional degree in landscape architecture. Landscape science also has significant overlap with botany, geology, ecology, hydrology, soil science and wildlife and habitat conservation, among a wide range of scientific disciplines.

Landscape science is collaborative, interdisciplinary work. Examples of the work within the scope of a landscape scientist would be ecological surveys, wildlife studies, planting studies, conservation, management, pollution mitigation (such as phytoremediation) and reclamation.

Environmental assessment is an important part of the work of landscape architects, and this involves preparing landscape and visual impact assessments, reports and, occasionally, appearing as an expert witness in public inquiries.

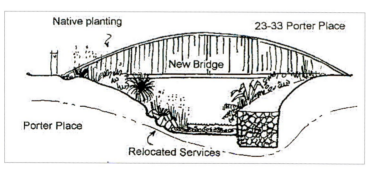

Manaaki Whenua Landcare Research sustainable drainage and biodiversity management
Landscape and environmental scientists are not always directly involved in design, but there is much communication between the two groups. It is important to study and document the effects of human interventions in the landscape so that future interventions can be more sensitive. Landscape science is often most complex in urban environments, and the project here shows how sustainable drainage channels were used in a housing development to improve the environmental health of not just the immediate area, but the whole region.

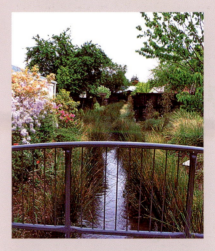

The Fundamentals of Landscape Architecture

CITIES AND TOWNS

'The garden discloses what the city ought to be.'
Colin Rowe

The work of landscape architecture is largely within an urban context. Urban environments, such as public squares, housing, streets and parks, make up the bulk of the work for many landscape practices. Landscape architects also establish urban strategy in documents such as masterplans, public realm strategies, urban design frameworks and urban design codes.

It is increasingly common for landscape architects to specialise in urban design and to call themselves urban designers. It is important to recognise that urban design is a discipline rather than a profession, and it is commonly held to represent the collaboration of architects, landscape architects and urban planners, and to exist at the intersection of these professions. One must be qualified in one of these three professions first before the additional title of urban designer is added. Many practitioners are now taking an additional degree in urban design.

Urban landscape architecture requires a willingness to work closely with other professions as well as a good understanding of all the forces that shape cities, from economics to politics to psychology.

Landscape urbanism has recently emerged as an additional discipline, and it seeks to highlight the importance of landscape architecture for determining urban form, seeing the landscape as the framework that defines cities.

StoSS Landscape Urbanism, New Bedford Masterplan
StoSS, headed by Chris Reed, is a particularly dynamic practice, and one of the few operating quite specifically in the field of landscape urbanism. The firm's philosophy is based in tying together social, cultural and ecological issues across the landscape. Like the Antonine Wall in Scotland (see pages 169), which allows a swathe of rural and lightly settled landscape to be addressed and considered along a linear stretch, in New Bedford two major Interstate Highway corridors become tools for large-scale urbanism.

The New Bedford Masterplan Phase 2 puts forth StoSS's plans to transform each of these highways into sequences of experiences that celebrate the entry into the city. Installations and civic gateways along the route reveal the workings of the local environment, from its physical and natural processes to people's relationship with it. As such, they use the language of the place to create a sense of arrival in New Bedford. Particular installations include a 'River Gate' at a crossing over the Acushnet River, a 'Wind Sock Gate' at the landing approach to the city's airport, and an 'Erratics Gate' that makes reference to the area's formation by massive glaciers and the resulting legacy of stone walls in the area.

GARDENS AND PARKS

'Gardens focus the art of place-making or landscape architecture in the way that poetry can focus the art of writing.'
John Dixon Hunt

Gardens and parks have historically formed the core of the services of landscape architects, though this is less and less the case, particularly with private gardens. Gardens are the basic unit of human inhabitation of the landscape, and they can be viewed as microcosms of the larger landscape. Landscape architects who are interested in garden design can certainly still find work in that area and the work is challenging and meaningful. A strong knowledge of plants is required, as well as the building blocks of landscape such as soils, geology, water, climate and topography. All the elements and practices of design, such as form, texture and colour come strongly to bear in gardens.

The green public spaces in which people gather, play and relax are crucial not just for human health and well-being, but also serve as important habitats for animals, including migratory birds. We are becoming increasingly aware of the importance of parks to assist with cleaning air and water, and for helping to moderate urban temperatures in the heat of summer.

Designing parks and gardens requires landscape architects to create construction drawings to show how elements are to be built and to provide planting plans for the design.

Cao Perrot Studios, Jardin des Hespérides, Quebec
Xavier Perrot and Andy Cao have offices in Paris and Los Angeles, and have become known internationally for creating gardens of ethereal beauty with exacting precision and skill. Indeed, the exceptional rigour with which they approach their work is essential to allowing the visitor to forget the fact of design and be transported by a garden. They designed the Jardin des Hespérides for the Metis International Garden Festival of 2006. The design voice of Andy Cao can clearly be heard, as the garden uses materials, scents and textures from his native Vietnam.

CONCLUSION

It seems in many ways that we are entering a future that is ever more uncertain, and the concerns that keep people awake at night are dreadful to contemplate and global in their reach. Climate change, coming crises in food and energy and economic uncertainty, highlight that we are reaching the limit of this fragile world's abundant, but finite, capacity to absorb our human impact. The antidote to anxiety is action, and the broad scope of the field of landscape architecture affords many opportunities for meaningful, positive action. We will see, more and more, a worldwide shift in politics and philosophy towards understanding and nurturing the landscape, and the professions of landscape architecture, planning and management will grow in size and importance as this occurs.

I hope that this book has given a taste of the great range of opportunities within landscape architecture. I recommend that the reader with specific interests and questions should take advantage of the books, contacts and resources listed in the next few pages.

If you have picked up this book because you are looking for a career that allows you a certain restless variety, amongst peers who won't laugh at you because you 'want to save the world', or even that you just want to leave the world a bit more beautiful in places, then I hope you may have found your calling amongst the projects, ideas and images here.

Hans Dieter Schaal, Burgerpark in Biberach an der Riß, 1999–2002
A house in the 18th century by the poet Christoph Martin Wieland is framed by poplars, water and light.

GLOSSARY

Access 1. *n.* A point of entry to a site or building. 2. *v.* to approach or enter.

Architectures, The. *n.* A convenient term for all the professions and disciplines concerned with the three-dimensional design of buildings and/or landscapes. This includes, and is not limited to, building architecture, interior architecture, landscape architecture, landscape planning, urban design and urban planning.

Axis *n.* A central spine along which a site or building design is organised. Elements to either side of the axis may or may not be symmetrical.

Axonometric *n.* A three-dimensional measured drawing with a bird's eye point of view. The term may be used to indicate any measured bird's-eye drawing or a specific projection with a 45-degree angle between the *x* and *z* axes.

Baroque *n.* A style of urban and park design that has extended well beyond its origins in the Renaissance. It is characterised by radiating streets or paths organised around focal points and vistas.

Biomorphic *adj.* Organically shaped. Generally refers to globular forms such as the 'kidney' shape so popular in the 1950s.

Brief *n.* An initial description of a project problem that defines the parameters within which the designer will work.

Built environment *n.* The landscape where it has specifically been shaped by human design or influence.

CAD *abbrev.* for: Computer-Aided Design. Software programs used as an aid to visualisation, presentation or drawings.

CHP *abbrev.* for: Combined Heat and Power. A distributed system of localised heat and power generation that allows communities energy independence and self-sufficiency.

Circulation *n.* The movement of people and vehicles through and around a site.

Climate change *n.* An overall and probably catastrophic change in average weather patterns that requires human and environmental adaptation through design and behavioural change.

Commission 1. *n.* The authority given to perform design work. 2. *v.* To give a design job to a chosen firm.

Community *n.* 1. A group of people with interests in common. 2. An inhabited area populated with people who have interests in common, at least in part because of geographic proximity to each other (propinquity).

Composition *n.* The arrangement of design elements in relation to each other, resulting in a pleasing unity.

Concept *n.* An idea. An abstract notion that serves to underpin a design proposal.

Contour *n.* An imaginary line traced upon the surface of the land at a single elevation that may be represented on a plan. Groupings of contours on a plan are used to indicate topography (see Topography).

Cultural landscape *n.* A landscape that has developed in a distinctive way over time due to human occupation and influence. The human experience will have been shaped in turn by the landscape.

Density *n*. A measure of the intensity of a site's occupation, both in terms of human population and buildings. The city of Hong Kong has very high density, both of buildings and people. The Sahara Desert has extremely low density.

Ecology *n*. The study of relations between organisms and the environment, and of natural systems.

Elevation *n*. The distance of a specific point on the land above or below either sea level or a fixed reference point. For elevation drawing, see Section elevation.

Environment *n*. 1. A setting or milieu for something or someone. 2. The overall systems of land, water, vegetation, wildlife etc. that comprise the setting for life on Earth.

Exploded axonometric *n*. A measured three-dimensional bird's-eye view that separates individual elements out into discrete layers.

Figure/ground *n*. An plan used for analysis that shows the relationship between built form and surrounding space. Generally buildings are shown as black masses, or 'figures', on a white 'ground'. If the figure/ground drawing is showing public open space, then the ground may extend into public buildings.

Genius loci *n*. Translates as 'the genius of the place'. The unique qualities of a place that should be taken into account and valued in a design for it.

GIS *abbrev*. for: Geographic Information System. A computer system that allows for complex mapping, analysis, layering and comparison of geographic data.

GPS *abbrev*. for: Global Positioning System. A computer system designed to assist terrestrial navigation and cartography. GPS employs satellite technology in combination with receivers to calculate position on the Earth's surface.

Historic conservation *n*. The work of designing for and protecting landscapes of historic and/or archaeological significance.

Isometric *n*. A three-dimensional measured drawing with a bird's eye point of view. A specific projection with a 30-degree angle between the *x* and *z* axes.

Landscape character *n*. The sum of all an area's attributes that result in its unique appearance and environment. Landscapes may have attributes in common, which allows them to be compared and contrasted with other similar landscapes.

Landscape management *n. v*. Care for and development of landscapes.

Landscape planning *n. v*. Development of policy and strategies for larger areas of landscape.

Landscape science *n*. The study and administration of processes and systems, both physical and natural, in ecology and the environment.

Land use *n*. The activity that takes place in a given area. Typical uses might include industry, housing, or playing field. Rarely, however, is any landscape used for one activity alone.

Massing *n*. The three-dimensional relationship between the physical bulk of buildings in a grouping and landscape elements such as trees and walls, and between buildings, landscape elements, and their immediate landscape.

Masterplan *n*. A plan or strategy for a complex development or environment and the supporting documents that detail how the plan will be costed, built, administered and managed.

Microclimate *n*. Average weather conditions in a small and specific area, such as the corner of a garden or the slope of a hill.

New town *n*. A development of housing, commerce, industry, transportation and all such elements of a standard town that is undertaken as a single, large-scale endeavour.

Orthographic projection *n*. Technical drawing. A measured scale drawing producing a 'true' representation of a site or object.

Perspective *n*. Realistic, three-dimensional drawings constructed with imaginary lines that converge in the background in what is called a 'vanishing point'. These lines give the picture depth, and often a horizon.

Photomontage *n*. A technique, akin to collage, for bringing disparate elements together into an often photorealistic image.

Place *n*. A space within the landscape that has acquired human meaning through human inhabitation.

Plan *n*. A two-dimensional measured horizontal drawing that places the viewer in an imaginary position above the site or object looking straight down at it without any distortion.

Plant palette *n*. 1. A selection of plants customarily used by a designer. 2. The full range of plants that it is possible or appropriate to grow in a specific area.

Portfolio *n*. A presentation, either digital or printed, intended to convey the skills and experience of an individual designer to a specific audience. Samples of work are included that are intended to display the range of a designer's capabilities, showing drawings in various media and skills with various computer applications.

Programme *n*. A series of steps, or a more complex dynamic interrelationship of elements that sets the parameters for a site's design. Programme balances the needs and requirements of both the site and the client.

Public realm *n*. Any landscape area or building interior that is free for the use of all people at all times. Usually used in an urban context.

Public space *n*. Any landscape area or building interior that is free for the use of all people at all times.

Representation 1. *n*. An image that stands for or symbolises an idea, concept or elements of the physical world. 2. *v*. The creation of such an image.

Scale *n*. The medium through which it is possible to create orthographic projections at a specific fraction of the full-size dimensions of a site or object. Scale is generally expressed as a fraction or a ratio.

Section *n*. A two-dimensional measured drawing showing the heights and widths of objects, and the distances between them, encountered on a vertical slice through the objects appearing on a plan.

Section elevation *n*. A section drawing showing not merely the object and relationships captured on the slice through the plan, but also everything appearing behind those elements looking in one direction.

Site *n*. An area that has been marked out for human use or action.

Site analysis *n*. The process of evaluating the characteristics that are listed in the site inventory.

Site inventory *n*. A list or an accounting of everything that exists on a site, establishing the context for analysis and design.

Site survey *n*. 1. An accurate record of a site's surface and its boundaries. 2. Site inventory.

Storyboard *n*. A technique, originating in film and animation, for showing a sequence of actions and/or experiences as a series of drawings.

SuDS *abbrev*. for: Sustainable Drainage Systems (formerly SUDS, abbrev. for Sustainable Urban Drainage Systems).

Sustainability *n*. The doctrine of ensuring that the design, construction and occupation of a site are completely in balance with its total context, including the environmental, sociological, cultural and economic considerations. Self-sufficiency, both individual and community, is usually at the heart of sustainability.

Synthesis *n*. The process of bringing analysis and concepts together to create design solutions for the problems that are posed by the brief.

Topography *n*. 1. The rise and fall of land and the natural and artificial features created by soil, rocks and buildings, and, in a more traditional sense, it also refers to the shape of the land created by the type of vegetation on the land. 2. The shape of the land and how it is described on maps or plans with contour lines.

Urban design *n*. The inter- and multi-disciplinary process of shaping spaces of human settlement.

Urbanism *n*. 1. Urban design 2. The study of all the various forces that shape urban spaces and activities.

Volume *n*. Individual landscape spaces, like vessels, have volume. This volume is defined and contained by the planes of space – the ground plane, the overhead plane, and the vertical plane (or, simply, the verticals).

Watershed *n*. A whole region that drains into a river or body of water.

CONTACTS AND USEFUL RESOURCES

GENERAL INFORMATION

These websites provide excellent basic or general information to those who are interested to learn more about landscape architecture. Each also provides useful links to other resources.

I Want to be a Landscape Architect
www.iwanttobealandscapearchitect.com

Garden Visit
www.gardenvisit.com

Land8Lounge
www.land8lounge.com

Landscape Information Hub
www.lih.gre.ac.uk

LarcExchange
www.larcexchange.com

Project for Public Spaces
www.pps.org

Resource for Urban Design Information (RUDI)
www.rudi.net

INTERNATIONAL ORGANISATIONS

There are many international organisations that are directly or indirectly concerned with the landscape, and these are a small selection of some of the more significant.

CELA Council of Educators in Landscape Architecture
www.thecela.org

EDRA Environmental Design Research Association
www.edra.org

IALE International Association for Landscape Ecology
www.landscape-ecology.org

ICOMOS International Council on Monuments and Sites
www.icomos.org

IFLA International Federation of Landscape Architects
www.iflaonline.org

ISOCARP International Society of City and Regional Planners
www.isocarp.org

IUCN International Union for the Conservation of Nature
www.iucn.org

UIA Union Internationale des Architectes
www.uia-architectes.org

UNEP United Nations Environment Programme
www.unep.org

UN Habitat United Nations Human Settlements Programme
www.unhabitat.org

EUROPEAN ORGANISATIONS

Europe is well served by networks and associations, both for professionals and students.

EFLA European Foundation for Landscape Architecture
www.efla.org

ELAN European Landscape Architecture Network
www.e-lan.org

ELASA European Landscape Architecture Students Association
www.elasa.org

CEU Council for European Urbanism
www.ceunet.org

Landscape Europe
www.landscape-europe.net

PROFESSIONAL ORGANISATIONS BY COUNTRY

For information about studying landscape architecture or practising in various countries, the best point of contact is the national professional organisation.

Only those organisations with websites are listed here. Other countries may be found listed at the International Federation of Landscape Architects website at *www.iflaonline.org*.

Argentina
(CAAP) Centro Argentino de Arquitectos Paisajistas
www.caapaisajistas.org.ar

Australia
(AILA) Australian Institute of Landscape Architects
www.aila.org.au

Austria
(ÖGLA) Österreichische Gesellschaft für Landschaftsplanung und Landschaftsarchitektur
www.oegla.at

Brazil
(ABAP) Associação Brasileira de Arquitetos Paisagistas
www.abap.org.br

Canada
(CSLAAAPC) The Canadian Society of Landscape Architects / L'Association des architectes paysagistes du Canada
www.aapc.ca

China
(CHSLA) Chinese Society of Landscape Architecture
www.chsla.org.cn

Czech Republic
(CZLA) Czech Landscape and Garden Society
www.szkt.cz

Denmark
(DL) Danske Landskabsarkitekter
www.landskabsarkitekter.dk

Finland
(MARK) Suomen Maisema-
arkkitehtiliitto Finlands
Landskapsarkitektförbund
www.m-ark.fi

France
(FFP) Fédération Française du
Paysage
www.f-f-p.org

Germany
(BDLA) Bund Deutscher
Landschaftsarchitekten
www.bdla.de

Greece
(PHALA) Panhellenic Association of
Landscape Architects
www.phala.gr

Hong Kong
(HKILA) The Hong Kong Institute of
Landscape Architects
www.hkila.com

Iceland
(FILA) Félag Islenskra
Landslagsarkitekta
www.fila.is

India
(ISOLA) Indian Society of Landscape
Architects
www.indianlandscape.net

Ireland
(ILI) Irish Landscape Institute
www.irishlandscapeinstitute.com

Italy
(AIAPP) Associazione Italiana di
Architettura del Paesaggio
www.aiapp.net

Kenya
(AAK) The Architectural Association
of Kenya
www.aak.or.ke

Korea
(KILA) Korean Institute of Landscape
Architecture
www.kila.or.kr

Latvia
(LAAB) The Latvian Society of
Landscape Architects
www.laab.lv

Malaysia
(ILAM) Institute of Landscape
Architects Malaysia
www.ilamalaysia.org

Mexico
(SAP) Sociedad de Arquitectos
Paisajistas de México, A.C.
www.sapm.com.mx

The Netherlands
(NVTL) Nederlandse Vereniging voor
Tuin-en Landschapsarchitektuur
www.nvtl.nl

New Zealand
(NZILA) New Zealand Institute of
Landscape Architects
www.nzila.co.nz

Norway
(NLA) Norske Landskapsarkitekters
Forening
www.landskapsarkitektur.no

Peru
(APP) Asociación Peruana de
Arquitectura del Paisaje
www.paiperu.org

Philippines
(PALA) Philippine Association of
Landscape Architects
www.pala.org.ph

Portugal
(APAP) Associação Portuguesa dos
Arquitectos Paisagistas
www.apap.pt

Puerto Rico
(CAAPPR) Colegio de Arquitectos y
Arquitectos Paisajistas de Puerto
Rico
www.caappr.com

Serbia
(UPA) Association of Landscape
Architects, Serbia and Montenegro
www.upa.org.yu

Singapore
(SILA) Singapore Institute of
Landscape Architects
www.sila.org.sg

Slovenia
(DKAS) Društvo krajinskih arhitektov
Slovenije
www.dkas.si

South Africa
(ILASA) Institute of Landscape
Architects of South Africa
www.ilasa.co.za

Spain
(AEP) Asociación Española de
Paisajistas
www.aepaisajistas.org

Sweden
(SA) Sveriges Arkitekter
www.arkitekt.se

Switzerland
(BSLA) Bund Schweizer
Landschaftsarchitekten und
Landschafts-architektinnen
www.bsla.ch

Thailand
(TALA) Thai Association of Landscape
Architects
www.talalandscape.org

Turkey
(UCTEA) Chamber of Landscape
Architects
www.peyzajmimoda.org.tr

United Kingdom
(LI) The Landscape Institute
www.thelandscapeinstitute.org

(SLIC) Student Landscape Institute
Council
www.slic.info

(UDG) Urban Design Group
www.udg.org.uk

United States of America
(ASLA) American Society of
Landscape Architects
www.asla.org

PROFESSIONAL JOURNALS

The breadth of the field of landscape
architecture means that there are
thousands of journals that are
pertinent to different areas. The
list below is a selection of some of
the best from across the range of
landscape architectural practice.

a+u Architecture and Urbanism
(Japan)
www.japan-architect.co.jp

ARQ Chile
www.puc.cl

Arquitetura & Urbanismo (Brazil)
www.piniweb.com.br

Chinese Landscape Architecture
www.jchla.com

Garden Design Magazine
www.gardendesign.com

Garten + Landschaft (Germany)
www.garten-landschaft.de

Green Places
www.landscape.co.uk/greenplaces/
journal

Harvard Design Magazine
www.gsd.harvard.edu/research/
publications/hdm

Horticulture Magazine
www.hortmag.com

Horticulture Week
www.hortweek.com

Jornal da Paisagem (Brazil)
www.jornaldapaisagem.unisul.br

Journal of Urban Design
www.tandf.co.uk/journals/
carfax/13574809.html

Journal of Urbanism
www.tandf.co.uk/journals/
titles/17549175.asp

Kerb: The Journal of Landscape
Architecture
www.kerbjournal.com

Landscape (UK)
www.wardour.co.uk

Landscape Journal
www.wisc.edu/wisconsinpress/
journals/journals/lj.html

Landscape Management
www.landscapemanagement.net

Landscape New Zealand
www.agm.co.nz

Landscape Research
www.tandf.co.uk/journals/
carfax/01426397.html

Landscapes/Paysages (Canada)
www.csla.ca

The Danish Architectural Press
(Denmark)
www.arkfo.dk

Metropolis
www.metropolismag.com

Native Plants Journal
www.nativeplants.for.uidaho.edu

New Urban News
www.newurbannews.com

Landscape Architecture Australia
www.aila.org.au/landscapeaustralia

Places Journal
www.places-journal.org

Regeneration and Renewal
www.regen.net

Sustainable Land Development
Today
www.sldtonline.com

Terrain.org
A Journal of Built and Natural
Environments
www.terrain.org

Topos: The International Review of
Landscape Architecture and Urban
Design
www.topos.de

Urban Design Journal
www.udg.org.uk/?section_id=5

Urban Green File (South Africa)
www.brookepattrick.co.za

BIBLIOGRAPHY

Bell, Simon. *Landscape: Pattern, Perception and Process*. E & FN Spon, London, 1999.

Campbell, Louise. *Phoenix: Architecture Art Regeneration*. Black Dog Publishing, London, 2004.

Corner, James and Maclean, Alex S. *Taking Measures Across the American Landscape*. Yale University Press, New Haven, 1996.

Cullen, Gordon. *The Concise Townscape*. The Architectural Press, Oxford, 1961, 1971.

Gehl, Jan and Gemzoe, Lars. *New City Spaces*. The Danish Architectural Press, Copenhagen, 2003.

Hunt, John Dixon. *Greater Perfections: The Practice of Garden Theory*. Thames & Hudson, London, 2000.

Jackson, John Brinckerhoff. *Discovering the Vernacular Landscape*. Yale University Press, New Haven, 1984.

Jellicoe, Geoffrey and Susan. *The Landscape of Man: Shaping the Environment from Prehistory to the Present Day*, Third Edition. Thames & Hudson, London, 1995.

Kostof, Spiro and Castillo, Greg. *The City Assembled: Elements of Urban Form through History*. Thames & Hudson, London, 1992.

Kostof, Spiro. *The City Shaped: Urban Patterns and Meanings through History*. Thames & Hudson, London, 1999.

Lynch, Kevin. *The Image of the City*. MIT Press, Cambridge, Massachusetts, 1960.

McHarg, Ian. *Design with Nature*. John Wiley and Sons, New York, 1995.

Moore, Charles W., Mitchell, William J., and Turnbull, William Jr. *The Poetics of Gardens*. MIT Press, Cambridge, Massachusetts, 1988.

Reed, Peter. *Groundswell: Constructing the Contemporary Landscape*. Museum of Modern Art, New York, 2005.

Schroder, Thies. *Changes in Scenery: Contemporary Landscape Architecture in Europe*. Birkhauser, Basel, 2001.

Simonds, John Ormsbee. *Landscape Architecture: A Manual of Site Planning and Design*. McGraw-Hill, New York, 1998.

Spirn, Anne Whiston. *The Granite Garden: Urban Nature and Human Design*. Basic Books, New York, 1984.

Treib, Marc, ed. *Modern Landscape Architecture: A Critical Review*. MIT Press, Cambridge, Massachusetts, 1993.

Tuan, Yi-Fu. *Space and Place: The Perspective of Experience*. University of Minnesota Press, Minneapolis, 1977.

Waldheim, Charles, ed. *The Landscape Urbanism Reader*. Princeton Architectural Press, New York, 2006.

Walker, Peter and Simo, Melanie. *Invisible Gardens: The Search for Modernism in the American Landscape*. MIT Press, Cambridge, 1994.

Weilacher, Udo, Dixon-Hunt, John and Bann, Stephen. *Between Landscape Architecture and Land Art*. Birkhauser, Verlag AG, Basel, 1999.

Zapatka, Christian. *The American Landscape*. Princeton Architectural Press, New York, 1995.

INDEX

ACKNOWLEDGEMENTS AND PICTURE CREDITS

For moral support, patience and love, I owe much to my family, especially my partner Jason.

I am grateful for the support of my colleagues at Kingston University, where I taught during the writing of this book, and I'm indebted in particular to Ed Wall, who provided invaluable feedback and support throughout the project. My new colleagues at the Writtle School of Design have also supplied an inspiring and ambitious environment in which to work and write.

The Landscape Institute has been tremendously enthusiastic and supportive, especially Paul Lincoln, who recommended that I write this book, and Sue Beard who is always ready with sage advice and knowledge. I have spent many hours in the Landscape Institute Library, and I'm grateful to Kate Lander, who helped get the project rolling in the very early stages, to Lesley Malone who arrived as librarian during the course of this work, and to Annabel Downs, Archivist, for her input and her humour.

Robert Rummey and Elizabeth Staveley at Rummey Design in Sevenoaks and London were immensely helpful and encouraging, despite a heavy workload to otherwise distract them.

Thanks are also due to Renée Last, Brian Morris and Caroline Walmsley at AVA Books whose guidance has been impeccable, and who have become champions for landscape architecture in the process of creating this book.

Anne Odling-Smee created superb designs with great empathy for the book's content.

Leonie Taylor researched and sourced imagery.

Chris Mayes helped me avoid any major missteps in history and ideas.

Index compiled by Indexing Specialists (UK) Ltd, www.indexing.co.uk

Finally, to all my friends in the US, who have cheered me on from a landscape far, far away, and my friends in the UK and Europe, who are near enough to prop me up in person.

Pages 9, 87–89: Courtesy of James Corner, Field Operations; Page 10: Image courtesy of Mikyoung Kim; Pages 12–13, 15, 25, 35, 38, 48, 81, 171–173: www. Shutterstock.com; Pages 14–19, 21, 23–25, 27, 33, 45, 66, 82, 95: www.iStock.com; Page 28: © José Fuste Raga/ Corbis; Pages 29, 41, 62–63, 65, 73, 146: Images courtesy of the author; Page 31: © Schlossverwaltung Hellbrunn 2008; Pages 32, 39: © Massimo Listri/CORBIS; Page 43: Thomas D. Church Collection (1997–2001) Environmental Design Archives, University of California, Berkeley; Page 47: Courtesy of Bernard Tschumi Architects; Pages 48–49, 129: Courtesy of West 8; Pages 51, 69: Courtesy of Margie Ruddick; Pages 52–53, 164–165: Courtesy of Mary Miss Studio; Pages 55, 56, 132, 177: Courtesy of Chris Reed, © Stoss Inc; Pages 58–59, 168–169: Courtesy of Land Use Consultants; Pages 60–61: Courtesy of Bjarne Aasen; Page 62: Courtesy of Arup; Pages 70–71: Courtesy of Murase Associates; Page 74: Courtesy of Lucy Smith; Pages 77, 119: © Shlomo Aronson; Pages 78–79: Courtesy of Shell and Gustafson Porter © Luc Boegly / Courtesy of Shell and Gustafson Porter © Claire de Virieu; Pages 84–85, 90–91: Courtesy of Ken Smith; Pages 93, 180–181: Courtesy of Hans Dieter Schaal; Page 97: Courtesy Oehme and Van Sweden; Pages 98, 166–167, 180–181: Courtesy of Wirtz International NV; Pages 101: Courtesy of Space Syntax; Page 103: © Hamilton-Baillie Associates Ltd; Pages 104–107: Courtesy of Olin; Pages 109–110, 115: Courtesy of Bo01 Malmo; Cover + Pages 112–113, 124-125, 136: Courtesy of Latz + Partner; Page 117: Courtesy of Ed Wall (sketchbook); Pages 117, 127, 133, 135, 139: Courtesy of Writtle School of Design; Pages 116, 120–121: Courtesy of Lucy White; Page 122: Courtesy of Gabriel Hydrick; Page 123: Courtesy of Rich Bensman; Page 131: Courtesy of Daphne Kao; Page 137: Courtesy of Daphne Kao and Ed Wall; Pages 140–163: Courtesy of Rummey Design; Page 174–175: Courtesy of Manaaki Whenua Landcare Research; Pages 178–179: Courtesy of Cao Perrot Studios.

Lynne Elvins/Naomi Goulder

Working with ethics
The Fundamentals
of Landscape
Architecture

194

The subject of ethics is not new, yet its consideration within the applied visual arts is perhaps not as prevalent as it might be. Our aim here is to help a new generation of students, educators and practitioners find a methodology for structuring their thoughts and reflections in this vital area.

AVA Publishing hopes that these **Working with ethics** pages provide a platform for consideration and a flexible method for incorporating ethical concerns in the work of educators, students and professionals. Our approach consists of four parts:

The **introduction** is intended to be an accessible snapshot of the ethical landscape, both in terms of historical development and current dominant themes.

The **framework** positions ethical consideration into four areas and poses questions about the practical implications that might occur. Marking your response to each of these questions on the scale shown will allow your reactions to be further explored by comparison.

The **case study** sets out a real project and then poses some ethical questions for further consideration. This is a focus point for a debate rather than a critical analysis so there are no predetermined right or wrong answers.

A selection of **further reading** for you to consider areas of particular interest in more detail.

Ethics is a complex subject that interlaces the idea of responsibilities to society with a wide range of considerations relevant to the character and happiness of the individual. It concerns virtues of compassion, loyalty and strength, but also of confidence, imagination, humour and optimism. As introduced in ancient Greek philosophy, the fundamental ethical question is *what should I do?* How we might pursue a 'good' life not only raises moral concerns about the effects of our actions on others, but also personal concerns about our own integrity.

In modern times the most important and controversial questions in ethics have been the moral ones. With growing populations and improvements in mobility and communications, it is not surprising that considerations about how to structure our lives together on the planet should come to the forefront. For visual artists and communicators it should be no surprise that these considerations will enter into the creative process.

Some ethical considerations are already enshrined in government laws and regulations or in professional codes of conduct. For example, plagiarism and breaches of confidentiality can be punishable offences. Legislation in various nations makes it unlawful to exclude people with disabilities from accessing information or spaces. The trade of ivory as a material has been banned in many countries. In these cases, a clear line has been drawn under what is unacceptable. But most ethical matters remain open to debate, among experts and lay-people alike, and in the end we have to make our own choices on the basis of our own guiding principles or values. Is it more ethical to work for a charity than for a commercial company? Is it unethical to create something that others find ugly or offensive?

Specific questions such as these may lead to other questions that are more abstract. For example, is it only effects on humans (and what they care about) that are important, or might effects on the natural world require attention too? Is promoting ethical consequences justified even when it requires ethical sacrifices along the way? Must there be a single unifying theory of ethics (such as the Utilitarian thesis that the right course of action is always the one that leads to the greatest happiness of the greatest number), or might there always be many different ethical values that pull a person in various directions?

As we enter into ethical debate and engage with these dilemmas on a personal and professional level, we may change our views or change our view of others. The real test though is whether, as we reflect on these matters, we change the way we act as well as the way we think. Socrates, the 'father' of philosophy, proposed that people will naturally do 'good' if they know what is right. But this point might only lead us to yet another question: *how do we know what is right?*

You
What are your ethical beliefs?

Central to everything you do will be your attitude to people and issues around you. For some people their ethics are an active part of the decisions they make everyday as a consumer, a voter or a working professional. Others may think about ethics very little and yet this does not automatically make them unethical. Personal beliefs, lifestyle, politics, nationality, religion, gender, class or education can all influence your ethical viewpoint.

Using the scale, where would you place yourself? What do you take into account to make your decision? Compare results with your friends or colleagues.

Your client
What are your terms?

Working relationships are central to whether ethics can be embedded into a project, and your conduct on a day-to-day basis is a demonstration of your professional ethics. The decision with the biggest impact is whom you choose to work with in the first place. Cigarette companies or arms traders are often-cited examples when talking about where a line might be drawn, but rarely are real situations so extreme. At what point might you turn down a project on ethical grounds and how much does the reality of having to earn a living affect your ability to choose?

Using the scale, where would you place a project? How does this compare to your personal ethical level?

01 02 03 04 05 06 07 08 09 10

01 02 03 04 05 06 07 08 09 10

Your specifications
What are the impacts of your materials?

In relatively recent times we are learning that many natural materials are in short supply. At the same time we are increasingly aware that some man-made materials can have harmful, long-term effects on people or the planet. How much do you know about the materials that you use? Do you know where they come from, how far they travel and under what conditions they are obtained? When your creation is no longer needed, will it be easy and safe to recycle? Will it disappear without a trace? Are these considerations your responsibility or are they out of your hands?

Using the scale, mark how ethical your material choices are.

Your creation
What is the purpose of your work?

Between you, your colleagues and an agreed brief, what will your creation achieve? What purpose will it have in society and will it make a positive contribution? Should your work result in more than commercial success or industry awards? Might your creation help save lives, educate, protect or inspire? Form and function are two established aspects of judging a creation, but there is little consensus on the obligations of visual artists and communicators toward society, or the role they might have in solving social or environmental problems. If you want recognition for being the creator, how responsible are you for what you create and where might that responsibility end?

Using the scale, mark how ethical the purpose of your work is.

01 02 03 04 05 06 07 08 09 10

01 02 03 04 05 06 07 08 09 10

198

Working with publicly owned spaces is an aspect of landscape architecture that involves the discipline with issues of politics, society and ethics. The creation or restoration of public parks and buildings, housing estates, city squares, infrastructure or coastlines is a multidisciplinary activity where decisions can have large-scale consequences. Projects often reflect social attitudes of the time towards nature, communities, integration and freedom of movement. The best interests of the public should ideally be maintained, but this might be difficult amongst conflicting pressures from financial interests or political reputations. Similarly, what might benefit the taxpayer may have an adverse impact on the natural environment. Having a clear ethical stance or code of conduct from the outset can be crucial to negotiating such conflicts with conviction. Consulting with the public or directly involving them with the design process is one possible route to pursuing a more inclusive, diverse and ethical approach to creating public spaces, but at the same time this might create feelings of animosity or be accused of being an act of tokenism that only incurs the need for more time and money.

Landscape architect Andrew Jackson Downing first voiced and publicised the need for New York's Central Park in 1844. Supporters were primarily the wealthy, who admired the public grounds of London and Paris and argued that New York needed a similar facility to establish its international reputation. The State appointed a Central Park Commission to oversee the development and in 1857 a landscape design contest was held. Writer Frederick Law Olmsted and English architect Calvert Vaux developed the Greensward Plan, which was selected as the winning design.

Before construction could start the designated area had to be cleared of its inhabitants, most of whom were poor and either African Americans or immigrants. Roughly 1600 people were evicted under the rule of 'eminent domain', which allowed the government to seize private property for public purposes.

Following the completion of the park in 1873 it quickly slipped into decline, largely due to lack of interest from the New York authorities. Times were also changing; cars had been invented and were becoming commonplace. No longer were parks to be used only for walks and picnics, but people now wanted spaces for sports.

In 1934, Fiorello LaGuardia was elected mayor of New York City and gave Robert Moses the job of cleaning up Central Park. Lawns and trees were replanted, walls were sandblasted, bridges were repaired and major redesigning and construction work was carried out (19 playgrounds and 12 ball fields were created). By the 1970s Central Park had become a venue for public events on an unprecedented scale, including political rallies and demonstrations, festivals and massive concerts. But at the same time the city of New York was in economic and social crisis. Morale was low and crime was high. Central Park saw an era of vandalism, territorial use and illicit activity. As a result several citizen groups emerged to reclaim the park and called for proper planning and management.

The outcome was the establishment of the office of Central Park Administrator and The Central Park Conservancy was subsequently founded. Central Park was redesigned with a revolutionary zone-management system. Every zone has a specific individual accountable for its day-to-day maintenance. As of 2007 the Conservancy had invested approximately US$450 million in restoration and management. Today, Central Park is the most visited park in the United States with around 25 million visitors annually.

What responsibility does a landscape architect have to ensure a public space is maintained once it is complete?

Was it unethical to evict people in order to build a public park? Would this happen today?

Would you have worked on this project?

Commissioned by clients to install barrier walls and private pathways that can keep out or discourage those who are unwanted, or hired to create private commercial experiences out of what may have been public space, many become complicit in structuring the urban language of separation.
Ellen Posner
(former architecture critic)
'Cities for a Small Planet'
The Wall Street Journal

Further reading

200

AIGA
Design business and ethics
2007, AIGA

Eaton, Marcia Muelder
Aesthetics and the good life
1989, Associated University Press

Ellison, David
Ethics and aesthetics in European modernist literature
2001, Cambridge University Press

Fenner, David EW (Ed.)
Ethics and the arts: an anthology
1995, Garland Reference Library of Social Science

Gini, Al (Ed.)
Case studies in business ethics
2005, Prentice Hall

McDonough, William and Braungart, Michael
'Cradle to Cradle: Remaking the Way We Make Things'
2002

Papanek, Victor
'Design for the Real World: Making to Measure'
1971

United Nations
Global Compact: The Ten Principles
www.unglobalcompact.org/AboutTheGC/TheTenPrinciples/index.html